The Ethics of Waste

The Ethics of Waste

How We Relate to Rubbish

GAY HAWKINS

ROWMAN & LITTLEFIELD PUBLISHERS, INC.
Lanham • Boulder • New York • Toronto • Oxford

ROWMAN & LITTLEFIELD PUBLISHERS, INC.

Published in the United States of America
by Rowman & Littlefield Publishers, Inc.
A wholly owned subsidiary of The Rowman & Littlefield Publishing Group, Inc.
4501 Forbes Boulevard, Suite 200, Lanham, Maryland 20706
www.rowmanlittlefield.com

P.O. Box 317, Oxford OX2 9RU, UK

British Library Cataloguing in Publication Information Available

Library of Congress Cataloging-in-Publication Data

Hawkins, Gay
  The ethics of waste : how we relate to rubbish / Gay Hawkins.
    p. cm.
  Includes bibliographical references and index.
  ISBN 0-7425-3012-4 (cloth : alk. paper) — ISBN 0-7425-3013-2 (pbk. : alk. paper)
    1. Waste minimization. 2. Environmental responsibility. 3. Refuse and refuse
  disposal—Moral and ethical aspects. I. Title.
  TD793.9.H38 2006
  178—dc22

                                                                    2005021924

Printed in the United States of America

♾™ The paper used in this publication meets the minimum requirements of American
National Standard for Information Sciences—Permanence of Paper for Printed Library
Materials, ANSI/NISO Z39.48-1992.

Contents

Preface

When you confess to writing a book about waste, people start telling you stories. Hilarious and horrifying stories about encounters with blocked drains; desperate searches through a very full garbage bin looking for one lost Barbie doll shoe; the almost new bed taken to a landfill after an acrimonious breakup. Waste can generate powerful emotions. And not just bodily or organic waste—things don't have to be slimy or foul smelling to disturb us. The empty Coke can just quietly biding its time can really upset the order of things when it's encountered on a hike into pristine wilderness. You've made all this effort to get to a place where the ugly, shit end of capitalism won't be present, only to discover that your quest has been futile. A bit of rubbish has found its way into paradise and exposed all your yearnings for purity as doomed to failure.

The simplest definition of waste is discarded, expelled, or excess matter. But the stories above show that this doesn't get anywhere near the minefield of emotions and moral anxieties that waste can provoke. Waste is much more than what we want to get rid of. While terms like "rubbish" or "litter" describe the random by-products of daily life, "waste" invokes a much more complicated set of meanings. When it is used to describe a certain category of things, like "nuclear waste" or "medical waste," the wasted material gestures back to the economy that produced it. When "waste" is used in a normative sense, as a category of judgment, meanings proliferate fast. We aren't meant to waste our time, our money, our efforts, our lives; we are advised to "waste not, want not." Waste is at the heart of so many moral economies that it's difficult to find any sense in which it isn't bad. To be unproductive or to excessively expend is a sign of poor discipline and irresponsible conduct. Minimizing waste in the interest of efficiency is regarded as evidence of an effective economy: industrial, moral, and psychic.

The paradox is that in among all this moral opprobrium being wasteful in the ways we live is encouraged, expected and, in many instances, impossible to avoid. Your DVD player breaks down after fifteen months of occasional use and the repairer says it will cost $150 to fix, *if* he can find the parts; "Cheaper to buy another one," he advises. Your children refuse to wear their siblings' outgrown, perfectly fine jeans because they aren't the latest fashion; they must have new ones—everybody else does! Explanations of how wasteful this is are met with a blank stare. In the commodity relations that touch every aspect of life, waste, as conspicuous consumption, is an invitation most find difficult to refuse. Not because they lack moral fiber but because this particular habit is embedded in the character of social life. Constant serial replacement works because a fashion system and certain forms of identity underwrite it. When who you are is thoroughly caught up with what you own—with the things you display on your body or in your home—conspicuous consumption becomes central to the cultivation of a self and to structures of social value and distinction.

Commodity cultures show how waste as a practice of excess can be free of negative connotations. The invitation to shop, shop, shop suppresses any mention of waste. The desire to possess and accumulate things is completely disconnected from the issue of how commodities are produced and where they end up once we decide they're valueless. Constant consumption is framed as an expression of personal freedom and choice. But the other side of it is the freedom to waste, to discard things that are still perfectly useful.

There's a moralism creeping into my account of commodity cultures that is hard to avoid. My aim in this book is not to moralize about waste. I don't think anyone who has access to television or a newspaper or a recycling bin needs to be reminded about the devastating effects of waste matter and of exploitative and wasteful economic practices on the planet. Nor do I want to use these brute realities as metaphors for the shape we're in—much as I like the biting precision of the term *affluenza*. Rather, I want to think about waste as a flexible category grounded in social relations. A category that acquires its meanings according to the different contexts and ways in which it has been historically put to work.

My interest is in the ways waste is implicated in the making of a self and particular ethical sensibilities. How does waste feature in our everyday habits and practices? We spend a fair amount of time each day managing waste: washing ourselves, going to the toilet, taking out the garbage, sorting out the packaging from the latest purchase into recyclable and nonrecyclable, taking the compost down to the garden, emptying the trash in our e-mail, picking out clothes for the charity bin. There's lots of different waste here—biological, material, informational—and lots of different techniques and bodily practices involved in eliminating it. There's also a whole swarm of thoughts and feelings about why these practices matter and what their effects are. Waste obviously has a vital role to play in the care of the self.

Feeling clean and purified are obvious outcomes of our everyday waste habits, but so too is feeling good. This sense of goodness, of having done the right thing for the environment, shows that contemporary waste habits have become connected to the practice of virtue or a sense of obligation to particular rules and moral codes. This experience is relatively new. The idea of recycling and composting as virtuous is a product of significant transformations in the ways waste has been framed. The problematization of waste as environmentally destructive is part of our recent history. It has informed numerous changes in governmental programs for waste management—particularly, mass education campaigns designed to change personal and domestic conducts. These campaigns have changed the ways we behave around waste, the meanings of wasted things—from rubbish to recyclables—and the moral economy of waste. They have implicated waste in the formation of new circuits of guilt and conscience and practices of self-regulation.

This book explores the intersections of habits, bodies, ethics, and waste matter. My curiosity about waste comes from a desire to understand how it might be possible to change ecologically destructive practices without recourse to guilt or moralism or despair. I feel all these things in relation to waste. And while these feelings have prompted me to change my behavior they can also immobilize me in certain ways. Sometimes they generate resentment, a sense of irritation that I have to rinse cans that I used to just chuck out. At other times these feelings can produce such an overwhelming sense of mourning for the state of the planet that it is difficult to find the energy and inspiration to sustain an ethical practice, let alone imagine better ones.

What often undoes these responses is waste itself. When you start writing a book about waste people start telling you stories *and* you start noticing waste. An innocent drive down the street on council trash night becomes an exercise in the recent history of home gym equipment. A trip to see the current Hollywood hit movie is disrupted by an extraordinary scene of dancing rubbish: How can an abandoned plastic bag have such an effect on you? A visit to a friend's house for dinner finds you going through the mess on their front verandah: "Are you really throwing this out?"

Waste is provocative, as much as we might like to think that it is just the redundant and rejected context to our lives, it can catch us in networks of obligation that reverberate across our bodies and invite us to live with it differently. I'm grateful to waste and the ways it's challenged me. And I'm grateful to the thinkers whose work has inspired me and helped me reflect on the ethics of waste, how they exist in the present, and how they might be transformed.

I am also grateful to numerous people and institutions for their help in completing this book. In the second half of 2003 I was awarded a writing fellowship from the Faculty of Arts and Social Sciences at the University of New South Wales (UNSW). This gave me the time and space to make significant progress. I presented drafts of two chapters at the Institute for Humanities at the University of Michigan while a visitor in the Department of English Language and Literature. On both occasions the comments and questions proved to be immensely stimulating and helpful, as was the intellectual environment of this lively department. Thanks to Elspeth Probyn I was able to present another chapter at the Wasted Bodies Seminar she organized in the Department of Gender Studies at the University of Sydney. Emily Potter invited me to present my work at the Environments and Ecologies Symposium in Adelaide. In both these forums the discussion and feedback were invaluable. Support for research came from the Australian Research Council Small Grants Scheme. Thanks to Carly Harper for her great research assistance and to Shaun Ankers and John Fox at Vermitech for information about worms. I'm also appreciative of my friends and colleagues in the School of Media and Communication at UNSW. They have tolerated my obsession with waste with patience and generosity. Julie Miller's calm and efficient administrative help was especially valuable.

This book has been written over a number of years, and during that time my thinking has been enriched by the ideas, support, and stimulation of a number of friends and colleagues. Thanks to Stephen Muecke, Liz Jacka, Simone Fullagar, Lee-Anne Hall, Anne Brewster, Maureen Burns, Emily Potter, Warwick Pearse, and Katrina Schlunke for reading drafts of various chapters and giving me thoughtful comments and proposals, as well as some tough editing suggestions. I've tried to take up most of their recommendations. Conversations with Ross Chambers and Patsy Yaeger were great for making me think again. Thanks to Kathy Gibson for introducing me to the work of William Connolly and Jane Bennett. And thanks to Akinori, Mituyo, and Mami Dansako for organizing my visit to the Kasaoka Recycling Centre in Japan and for being so generous and helpful during my time there.

For ongoing intellectual generosity and friendship I particularly want to thank David Halperin and Kane Race. Kane kept me up to date with contemporary theory and continually challenged me to take my thinking further. His comments on several chapters were incisive, as were innumerable lively conversations in which he helped me figure out what I was trying to do. His help teaching with me during the period of this book was great and made the classes so much better. Thanks, especially, to David, who has supported this project in so many ways. He knew what it was about long before I did. Our long and wonderful conversations by e-mail and in person, and his astute comments on my work, helped deepen my understanding and appreciation of Foucault's work on ethics, and see how it could be used to think about the ways we live with waste. He also facilitated two visits to Ann Arbor, where he provided me with the most idyllic conditions to write and think. To be able to work in such beautiful surroundings was a gift that helped this project enormously; his hospitality, generosity, and friendship are immensely appreciated.

I write in the context of a family, extended and immediate. My sisters, Merry and Rob; brother, Andy; and parents, Pam and Jim, have always supported my work—despite all the jokes—and I am grateful for their love, humor, and encouragement. I became fascinated with waste not long after the death of my father. I'm not sure what the connection is between the profound loss of a loved parent and small everyday losses like putting out the garbage, but I'm sure there is one. Endings, big and small, make you think about transience and how to live with loss in ways that affirm life. I thank Jim for all the

lessons in living well that he gave me, and for teaching me about the productive power of grief. Thanks, finally, to Nina, Louis, and Warwick who've lived
with the day-to-day reality of this book. My children have tolerated my dis-
traction with humor and goodwill. Their love and sense of fun kept my feet
on the ground and reminded me of the messiness of everyday life. Warwick
Pearse has been always encouraging and supportive; his kindness, sharp intel-
lect, and unfailing patience inspire respect and enormous thanks for the life
we share.

1

An Overflowing Bin

The garbage bin is already full and there are two more days until pickup. It smells. And it's in your way. Before you begin pushing and shoving or clandestine dumping in another bin—what if you stopped and wondered about the contents of the bin? Let your waste register as more than just a nuisance. Perhaps you'd feel disgusted at its messy visibility, or guilty about the amount of rubbish you generate, or annoyed that government waste services have been cut back in the name of budget cuts or environmental reform. Whatever the response, in that momentary flicker of feeling waste is making a claim on you.

When waste is noticed something shifts in the mundane landscape of domestic habits. The stench and confusion of the garbage bin can no longer be ignored—that rubbish needs some attention! In cultures that pride themselves on being technologically "advanced" catching a glimpse of the brute physicality of waste signals a kind of failure. After all, dual-flushing toilets and garbage contractors and In-Sink-Erators are meant to protect us from our waste; to hide the disgusting and the valueless with streamlined efficiently. This is how the elimination of waste became a marker of civilized modernity. And this is how the elimination of waste became implicated in the formation of a certain kind of person with distinct habits and beliefs as to what constitutes waste and how to get rid of it.

As much as putting out the garbage may feel like one of the most ordinary and tedious aspects of everyday life, it is a cultural performance, an organized

sequence of material practices that deploys certain technologies, bodily techniques, and assumptions. And in this performance waste matter is both defined and removed; a sense of order is established and a particular subject is
made. Waste, then, isn't a fixed category of things; it is an effect of classification and relations.

There's nothing new in this claim; Mary Douglas made it years ago in her
celebrated book *Purity and Danger*.[1] For any study of waste this book is of singular importance. It shows how the structuring capacities of culture come to
classify things as waste. Douglas denaturalizes dirt and waste and places them
firmly within the terrain of cultural rituals and their symbolic meanings. She
shows how the values of purity and danger become lodged in specific material forms and that dirt is not outside of order but what makes systems of order visible. Who could forget her most quotable quote, "Where there is dirt
there is system"?[2]

But there is only so far that you can get decoding a culture by going
through the garbage. At some point the gritty materiality of waste gets under
your fingernails, and the limit of classification and social construction is felt.
The mountains of cheap and broken consumer durables signify an economy
utterly dependent on disposability. The greasy fast food packaging reveals the
decline of home cooking. Waste becomes a social text that discloses the logic
or illogic of a culture. It becomes subordinated to human action, a slave to desire and manipulation. In the demand to show how waste is a result of cultural
practices—from religious taboos to consumer capitalism—the active connections between humans and wasted material in which *both* are produced are
hard to see. The action seems to flow all one way. Waste is reduced to a product of culturally and historically variable human practices; what we want to
get rid of tells us who we are.

This is true. But what we want to get rid of also *makes* us who we are. Social constructionism generally begins with the binary of waste versus human;
these determinate forms are the starting point for analysis. What becomes
harder to see is the actual movement of sociality. Or the process whereby
waste emerges and becomes recognizable and representable as the dead matter that affirms our living subjectivity, or sense of self. Sociality foregrounds
how waste becomes present to us, how it is encountered and experienced. Its
focus is on relations and interaction. And it is in the dynamics of these relations that it is possible to see the mutual constitution of human subjects and

inanimate wasted objects. These relations are culturally mediated; they don't take place in some presocial zone called raw experience. Sociality, then, is a field of emergence that Brian Massumi has described as "open-endedly social. It is social in a manner 'prior to' the separating out of individuals and the identifiable groupings that they tend to box themselves into."[3]

If human waste relations are dynamic, open-ended social entities, in the sense that new meanings and practices are always immanent—the ethical and political question is, how might new waste practices emerge? How might a different ethos of waste surface that is less destructive of the planet? These are the questions I explore in this book.

But as soon as I mention "the planet" there is an automatic expectation that I will launch into an account of the global waste crisis. This is not my intention. Though the politics of the environment inform and to a large extent motivate this book, I want to open up another way of making sense of waste beyond the trope of environmentalism. My concern is with our most quotidian relations with waste, what they mean and how they might change. I've started with the garbage bin and I pretty much want to stay there, though I will be making some detours to the bathroom and the open landfill. I want to think about the habits and practices that shape what we do with waste. How waste is implicated in embodiment and styles of self, the norms and codes that underpin waste management, and how these might, or might not, register as ethical obligations.

A lot can happen when waste is noticed, and thinking about the effects of the acute attention waste can sometimes provoke is another aim of this book. When I first began work on it I turned to psychoanalytic explanations of disgust and abjection as an important source.[4] This proved to be of limited use. While psychoanalysis is useful for explaining the visceral power of disgust in relation to bodily waste—the ways contact with shit or blood or pus can horrify and overwhelm us—most of the waste we encounter is not bodily and nor is it experienced as abjecting. The detritus of urban life congealed in gutters or dumped on the street doesn't destabilize the self. It just hangs around largely ignored. The centrality of abjection in accounts of the self-waste relation seems too ahistorical and subjectivist; too blind to the social and political frames that mediate how all waste is subject to classification. The focus on waste as a threat to the psyche ignores how historical changes in the micropractices of the self influence unconscious orientations to the disgusting. Psychoanalysis doesn't help make sense of the shifting place of waste in everyday life and material culture; how our ordinary encounters with it are implicated in the making of a self and an object world. It reduces waste to a phobia, understanding it only as a threat to self-certainty.

Waste's materiality is not the only thing that gets left behind in this approach. So too does any recognition of the self's creation in and through relations with waste matter. Waste doesn't just threaten the self in the horror of abjection, it also *constitutes* the self in the habits and embodied practices through which we decide what is connected to us and what isn't. Managing its biological or material reality is part of the way in which we organize our self and our environment, keep chaos at bay. This is why styles of waste disposal are also styles of self and why waste management, in all its cultural mutations, is fundamental to the practice of subjectivity. It is part of the way in which we cultivate sensibilities and sensual relations with the world; part of the way we move things out of our life and impose ethical and aesthetic order. No matter how insignificant putting out the garbage may seem, the way we do it reflects an ethos, a manner of being. And, as Michel Foucault has shown, an ethos is intimately connected with ethics; it is how a manner of being becomes implicated in the conduct of bodies.[5]

Of course this shift from the big dramas of the psyche to a focus on relations, habits, and ethics could become just another version of subjectivism that also sidelines waste. This is a danger I am well aware of. In the concern to understand the actions and practices that shape what becomes classified as waste and how it will be managed, waste will not necessarily get much chance to speak for itself. This is not to give waste a spurious autonomy. Rather, it is to be aware of the problem of subordinating waste to the vagaries of human uses and social construction so that it is difficult to capture the actual processes whereby something is perceived as waste and then rejected. I want to avoid this by focusing on how waste mediates relations to our bodies, prompts various habits and disciplines, and orders relations between the self and the world. This implicates waste in the action of ethics and embodiment as a key player. By paying constant attention to how waste impresses itself on us phenomenologically, I want to foreground the relational processes that bind us to waste even as we seek to be free of it. To reduce waste to an effect of human action and classification is to ignore the materiality of waste, its role in making us act; the ways in which waste is *both* a provocation to action and itself a result of that action. I take my lead from Bill Brown's account of the relational dynamics between persons and things. He argues that habits constitute the material world for the perceiving subject at the same time as they constitute the self. And in this process the possibility of an unnerving conflation between nature and culture, subject and object, and what we call persons and what we call things is ever present.[6]

This focus on minor acts and habits might seem trivial and indulgent in the face of a world drowning in garbage, but it opens up another way of thinking about waste that many forms of environmentalism have nurtured but never seriously analyzed. In the familiar slogan "Think globally, act locally" we have been urged to start with our own backyards, to save the earth by transforming our everyday practices. Choosing a paper bag rather than a plastic one, composting, recycling, all indicate important shifts in our relationship to waste matter, how we manage it, and how guilty or righteous it can make us feel.

There is no doubt that over the last thirty years, in the face of escalating amounts of waste, the rules surrounding putting out the garbage in late capitalist countries have changed. The question is: What are the impacts of this? At the level of daily experience the impacts are not as insignificant as they may seem. For a start, waste has been problematized, it has become a domain of life in which our taken for granted practices have been subjected to scrutiny and deemed in need of new attention and care. The rise of governmental campaigns imploring us to "reduce, reuse, recycle" haven't just implicated our everyday household practices in the global waste crisis, they have also implicated our bodies. In problematizing what we should do with our waste, these campaigns have also subjected *who* we are and *how* we should be in the world to scrutiny. It is impossible to change waste practices without implicating the self in a process of reflexivity, without asking people to implicitly or explicitly think about the way they live. This is the terrain of ethics, or the terrain of ethics that I am interested in. It links the historical specificity of moral codes and ideals with an embodied sensibility, with repeated practices and habits that shape how our bodies feel and the forms of reason that make these actions and affects meaningful. And in these changes in the governmental rules surrounding putting out the garbage waste has also changed; it has been revalued and recoded from rubbish to recyclable resource, it has moved from the bin to the compost heap, it has insinuated itself into our lives in different ways and with different effects.

However, recognizing a moral code and living it out are not automatic. Moral injunctions are not necessarily what underpin laudable acts. Many people have changed their waste practices because they have simply had no choice. Changes in local waste removal services, punitive measures, and economic imperatives have all coerced people into modifying their practices. They have also, no doubt, generated a sense of resentment and irritation at yet another incursion of the government into private life and domestic space. When people complain about not even being able to chuck things away without "the state" or "mad greenies" breathing down their necks they are experiencing changes in the administration of waste as a form of repressive power. They are not expressing a sense of obligation to their rubbish. Rather, they are expressing a victimized anger and frustration at underserved restrictions on their individual right to make as much waste as they please.

But resentment is only one response to these changes. Many evaluations of the implementation of more sustainable domestic waste practices document a deep moral attachment to these practices, a sense that people are concerned and willing to do their bit for the environment. This response shows not only that environmental campaigns that connect the global waste crisis to aspects of everyday life have resonated with sections of the population, but also that people have agreed to act on themselves, to change their habits. When people recycle or compost or refuse the plastic bag because they feel that this minor gesture will make a difference, they are accepting their obligations not just to the planet but to waste. They are enacting a different relation to waste, letting it register in the dimension of the ethical.

Big deal! As if that's going to change the catastrophe of ecological destruction; the global trade in waste from north to south; the excesses of unregulated, dirty capitalist production; or the obscenity of overconsumption. Recycling is just another opportunity for the righteous middle class to bleat on about how good they are, how virtuous they feel sorting the paper from the glass.

I can set down this vitriolic response with ease because I've heard it plenty of times when speaking at various environmental forums. And, rather than get defensive, I want to take these critiques seriously. While I accept much of their content I don't accept how they frame the political, or their blindness to questions of bodies, ethics, and the materiality of waste. In many senses I think this response is part of the problem. The dismissal of changes in personal practices as tokenism perpetuates the idea that politics is restricted to macroassemblages like the state or capitalism, and that real social transformation is possible only via wholesale revolutionary change. This approach doesn't just oppose the personal to the political, making it difficult to see the multiplicity of relations between these spheres. It can also, too easily, lapse into creating moralistic blueprints for changes in consciousness. These moral imperatives take no account of how bodies and feelings are implicated in thinking, often below the threshold of conscious decision making.

In contrast to this I want to investigate politics as a process of "active experimentation."[7] According to political philosopher Paul Patton, these experimental practices are played out *in between* large-scale political and economic institutions and the subinstitutional movements of affect, desire, and minor practices.[8] If active experimentation involves minor practices and the intensities of the body, then the everyday actions of cultivating a self would seem to be crucial for understanding how new waste habits and sensibilities might emerge.

My theorizations of politics adopt this poststructuralist perspective precisely because it is attentive to the relations between styles of embodiment and various regimes of power.[9] Poststructuralism's rejection of totalizing conceptions of control leads to a focus on the qualitative dimensions of deviant minor practices and how they can make trouble for all sorts of normativity. And it is precisely in these minor practices, like dealing with your waste, that experiments with new practices and sensibilities are most needed and most possible. William Connolly puts it like this: "Micropolitics and relational self-artistry shuffle back and forth among intensities, feelings, images, smells, and concepts, modifying some of them and the relays connecting them, opening up, thereby, the possibility of new thinking and alterations of sensibility."[10]

WASTED ENVIRONMENTS

Feeling uneasy about the structure of much environmentalist critique does not mean that I can avoid analyzing it. When it comes to waste, environmentalism's discursive impacts are significant. Environmentalism in all its varieties dominates representations of wasted things. And while some of these representations are positive, most are not. This broad discursive field has to accept full responsibility for using waste to stage the destruction of the planet. While it's easy to say I want to take a different approach to thinking waste, clearing a space for this has to begin with a careful investigation of how we already *know* waste. Existing representations don't just use waste to organize our fears about the end of nature; they also limit how we might respond to this. Fredric Jameson is absolutely right to point out that it's easier to imagine the destruction of the earth and of nature than the destruction of capitalism.[11] Our imaginations are overflowing with the horror of waste.

In much environmentalist discourse both humans and nature are configured as sites of loss. Nature is represented as the passive victim of gross exploitation and contamination, a realm of lost purity and sanctity. Humans, meanwhile, are alienated from the natural world, having lost their connection to the physical environment on which their very survival depends. The modern world is a place of dearth and meaninglessness; it has lost touch with community and with noninstrumental forms of reason. Everything is rationalized and calculable, systems of meaning have fractured and fragmented to the point at which people experience an absence of belief. Little wonder, then, that in much mainstream environmental politics waste is a central character in an already well-established disenchantment story.[12] Dumping waste is an expression of contempt for nature. Humans establish their sense of mastery over and separation from a passive desacralized nature by fouling it. The story then goes on to show how this has involved a profound shift in moral outlook from a more connected interaction with nature, in which the status and classification of waste was vastly different (perhaps there wasn't even such a category?), to our current state, in which global pollution and gross wastefulness, or "first world affluenza," signal a profound moral bankruptcy.

What are the effects of these familiar disenchantment stories? Obviously, they are various and complex. I just want to single out those that are relevant to the question of waste and how it is configured. Disenchantment stories shape the representations through which we make sense of the world; they are performative.[13] Our consciousness is full of these stock images, symbols and metaphors that form a kind of waste social imaginary. This imaginary provides a set of frameworks and ideas that operate in the background to our everyday practices. How that background is experienced is eminently variable; it might lurk as a constant source of guilt or sadness or it might be completely unacknowledged. Social imaginaries are akin to the operations of "discourse" or "mentality." They shape how we come to know and do things, the terms in which the world is made meaningful, but their presence is muted or backgrounded by the effects of embodiment and naturalization.[14]

Social imaginaries play a crucial role in the formation of our subjective understandings of waste and the environment. When we hear stories of dying rivers or see images of mountains made of garbage, nature is framed as dead or definitely on its last legs, and it's difficult not to feel a sense of despair or grief. While the political intention of these stories might be to shock us into action, their impact is often overwhelming and immobilizing. They can perpetuate the very relation to nature they seek to challenge: alienated distance and disinterest. When the exploitative force of economic power and human destruction is so overcoded why bother contesting it? You may as well just keep shopping.

My point is not that we need some positive messages as a counterbalance to current waste social imaginaries that will reenchant nature and inspire us. Social marketing has already discovered that feel good messages are more effective than feel bad. Rather, my point is that the very terms in which the culture-nature relation is framed in much environmentalism limit how new relations might be imagined. Disenchantment stories presume a fundamental dualism between human culture and nonhuman nature. No matter how they configure the relation between the two sides, each ultimately stands as ontologically distinct from the other. Each is seen as possessing an essential material difference from the other. This dualistic thinking inhibits any serious consideration of the specificities of waste and our relations with it. It posits a fixed identity for things that has to be protected if that identity is to remain pure. In the opposition of humans to nature that disenchantment stories sustain, waste functions *not* as what undoes this opposition but as what contaminates both sides. The capacity of humans to destroy nature with their waste renders them morally bankrupt, and the capacity of nature to function as a dumping ground renders it passive and denatured. The destruction of paradise happened not when Adam took a bite of the apple but when he dropped the core on the ground.

Waste can only be bad in this framework; it can only function as that which destroys the purity of both sides of the opposition. It is the thing that has to be eliminated in order to reestablish the essential identity and difference of each category. This tendency to blame waste uses a moral framework to explain the effects of destruction and contamination. Waste makes us feel bad, its presence disgusts and horrifies us, it wrecks everything—in these familiar sentiments badness is located in the object that disrupts purity rather than in the relation between the person having the affect and that object. In the quest to purify, which Bruno Latour describes as a typically modern strategy, waste has no generative capacities, only destructive ones.[15] No wonder it is so easy to use waste to stage our anxieties about the collapse of purified categories and clear boundaries.

Yet, as Latour also argues, purification goes hand in hand with the rise of translation, or the emergence of hybrid categories that are mixtures of nature and culture. The greater the demand for sharp distinctions between nature and culture, the more inevitable it becomes that an increasing number of things will not fit easily into either category. Could we think of waste as evidence of translation, as part of this proliferation of hybrids? It certainly shows us how mixed up the categories of culture and nature are, how everything contains elements of both. The abandoned car body rotting quietly in the landscape is alive with the activity of corrosion, it's become a habitat, it looks perfectly at home, it's both organic and machinic. The shifting and contingent meanings for waste, the innumerable ways in which it can be produced, reveal it not as essentially bad but as subject to relations. What is rubbish in one context is perfectly useful in another. Different classifications, valuing regimes, practices, and uses, enhance or elaborate different material qualities in things and persons—actively producing the distinctions between what will count as natural or cultural, a wasted thing or a valued object.

If disenchantment stories deny the complexity of waste at the same time as they blame it for contaminating both culture and nature how, then, do they imagine political change? What sorts of ethico-political strategies do they propose for saving both humans and the nonhuman world? In some versions of environmentalism the strategy is to get rid of the bad thing altogether. Banish waste from the new ecological order, because when humans understand their profound connections with a resacralized nature there will be no need for waste, it will become meaningless. Nothing will be wasted; it will be reused and reintegrated into the cycle of life and endless renewal. This approach idealizes nature as a transcendent entity excluding any relation to the immanent realm of bodies and dirt.[16]

But would a different culture in which we lived in harmony with nature do away with waste altogether? Doesn't this simply reproduce the idea of waste as phobic objects, as essentially bad? When people declare that there should be no such category as waste a niggling question remains: Don't we need it? What about the question of otherness or alterity? Isn't the demarcation of a world outside the self how we come to know who we are? Isn't the physical world and its alterity the "very basis for accepting otherness as such"?[17] Versions of environmentalism that emphasize merging with nature make it difficult to understand the function of separation as a distinct relation. Surely, what we reject is as important as what we identify with. Denying the possibility of separation in favor of connection does not allow for the possibility of having different relations with things that we frame as ontologically other. It forecloses the possibility of creating better ways of living with things that we reject as both different and redundant to our lives.

Ultimately, this vision of political change does not help me think about how our everyday ethical relations with waste might be transformed. It privileges a sacred nature as the impetus or motivation for change, and this displaces any serious consideration of how it might actually be *waste*, rather than "nature" or "the environment," that triggers new actions, that inspires us.

But the sacralization of nature is only one scenario for political change; there are plenty of others that are more modest and more familiar because they are the stuff of social marketing in the name of "environmental awareness and education." How do these campaigns represent waste? How do they configure the political? My aim here is not detailed genealogy. It is simply to examine the place of these strategies in framing or reframing our relations with waste. Across all the different genres of social marketing aimed at changing everyday waste management the mode of address presumes an autonomous subject in possession of free will and reason. This subject is seen as the owner of certain beliefs, opinions, and imaginings that need to be discarded and replaced by better, more ecologically sustainable ones. You might believe that empty bottles and newspapers are worthless rubbish, but they are really potential resources. You might regard food scraps as repulsive decaying matter, but they could be feeding your garden. The waste-making subject is invited to change his or her mind about the status of rubbish and then voluntarily transform his or her actions. These requests for change don't exist in a vacuum. They are meaningful only because of the wider context of disenchantment narratives that are deployed to morally problematize existing practices and beliefs, to justify changes—do it for the environment! And to offer the subject the experience of virtue when he or she does.

We are in the realm of voluntarism here and the assumption that opinions and beliefs are possessions that can be replaced with an act of will. The problem with this approach is that it represents reason as an exclusive property of the mind and denies the place of the body in modes of knowledge. Beliefs and opinions are embodied, they are inscribed in the ways we behave, experience, and feel. Any appeal to change our ways of living that does not take account of how we *feel* rather than just think about waste, that ignores bodies and the affective sphere, will be seriously impoverished. Responsibility and bodily responses are inextricably linked; modifications in reason alone will not change the character of social life.

Similarly, the invocation in many environmental campaigns of an abstracted "nature in crisis" that we are now morally obliged to rescue can impose senses of duty and obligation on the waste-making subject that can easily slide into resentment. Campaigns driven by the logic of moral imperatives can trigger victimization or despair: a sense that the world is unfairly imposing restrictions on your freedom and individuality; or a feeling of being impossibly overburdened with too many things clamoring for your sympathy. But it's not just the fact of people experiencing an excess of moral claims—or *compassion fatigue*, to use a trendier term—it is also the way in which these claims are made. When nature is represented as dying we are inevitably confronted with finitude. Even when this message is tempered with images of beauty and abundance or yet another spectacular documentary on whales, it takes only one newspaper report on the last three remaining brown-nosed wombats to get that sinking feeling again.

Witnessing nature's demise inevitably reminds us of our own. Whether this is acknowledged, even unconsciously, is impossible to guarantee. The forces of repression are powerful, especially in relation to that which threatens us most. It is easy to remain blind, to turn away, when we have so many fictions to keep death at bay: arrogant self-centeredness, nihilism. Then there is the option of converting the thing that reminds you of mortality into an object of contempt, converting the anxiety and vulnerability that something triggers in you into resentment, and thereby managing its threat—or thinking that you are. Environmental education strategies that identify waste as one of the key culprits in the demise of nature walk a knife edge between activism and resentment. Rather than inspiring positive action and generosity they can easily fuel a politics of fear and loathing, a cavalier disregard for nature that is often expressed through defensive reassertions of its status as a resource, as that which exists simply to remind humans of their superiority.

While environmental hard-liners reject educational approaches on the basis that they individualize what are really structural and institutional problems—thereby letting government and capital off the hook—my concern is with how a politics based on the imperative to reform the self in the name of nature can easily slide into moralism or resentment, distracting attention from how we actually live with waste and blinding us to the ubiquity of ethical work. In the appeal to make a grand gesture and do your bit to save the world, not only is nature once again subordinated to humans but the absolute ordinariness of managing waste is lost in a haze of righteousness.

Poor waste; environmentalism infuses it with a metaphysical dimension that makes it stand for death. Images and stories about its horrifying presence are used so constantly to stage our fears about the end of the world that its vital place in the care of the self and everyday life is consistently overlooked. In this book I want to redress this situation, to give waste the attention it deserves. My motivation is different from environmentalism in the sense that I do not see a closer analysis of our waste relations as a chance to get in touch with nature. I don't want to explain the need for changes in ways of managing waste in terms of fear and moral imperatives. Nor do I want to recuperate waste, invert its negative value to positive—though I do want to consider examples of its generative role. Standing on the edge of a landfill gives me nausea, not inspiration. Rather than rail against the effects of excessive consumption and a disposable culture (which I could easily do) or let my melancholy take over, I want to take notice of all those abandoned things. I want to think about the complexity of our relations with the material world that wasted things carry as traces on their scratched and broken surfaces. I want to investigate the ways in which objects become waste, the practices of valuing and classification that render them useless. I want to consider the historically specific network of political and cultural relations that organize the open landfill, the sewer, and the recycling bin as distinct technologies of waste management whose effects reverberate across our bodies in our daily rituals of dealing with our selves and our rubbish. The minute you start paying attention to waste a different relation with it is enacted; the chapters in this book enact that attention. They examine the effects of noticing waste, letting it confront us not as worthless detritus but as provocative things that just might make us consider what we do.

HABITS AND ETHICS

How then to think about waste not as phobic objects but as things we are caught up with? Things that are materialized or dematerialized through actions, things that work on us and help us constitute a self? Focusing on how waste figures in our relations with our body and the world means taking seriously dispositions and sensibilities around waste. This makes it possible to see how *other* relations might surface that make new claims on us, that inaugurate different habits. Recycling and composting are already doing this in their own small way. In the demand to handle our empty bottles or newspapers differently, our relations with these formerly useless things have changed. They have now become residual resource and we have become "environmentally aware." The ritual of rinsing and sorting has produced a new network of obligations and identities that show that the material specificities of waste are never fixed, and neither is the ethical constituency that feels implicated in it. Waste and bodies and habits are all open to immense variation, and in the emergence of new waste habits, an experiment with another social imaginary, whether it's explicitly identified or not, lurks in the background.

What then are habits and how are they implicated in the formation of an ethical sensibility? Habits are bodily dispositions. They are the way a body is organized and moves; the way corporeality has a social and cultural memory. Pierre Bourdieu describes habits as practical techniques based on a nonspontaneous principle of spontaneity.[18] They are nonspontaneous because memory, social circumstance, repetition, and environment shape how our spontaneous responses and practices emerge. Habits emerge in the relational imprints of meaning back and forth among levels of the body and its environs; their sedimentation confronts us as a kind of second nature. Habits and their repeated performance help form identity, they remind us that a self is made through actions and that different bodies and selves emerge in different practices.

My aim is not to moralize habits, to insist that we change our bad practices. I don't think that bringing morality into play with habits gets you very far. It simply infuses habits with the language of compulsion and demands that we call up our conscience and free will and control ourselves. Habits don't work like that. Habits have a materializing power on both persons and things. They bind us to the world at the same time as they blind us to it. And this is the problem and the possibility of habits: when they break down, when something goes wrong in their routine operation, we are launched into a new relation with the world. A moralized language of habit assumes that these new relations come from a rational self who has "seen the light." My claim is that waste and our interconnections with it, rather than abstract human reason, might have more of a role to play in disrupting habits than we ever give it credit. The waste that suddenly claims our attention, maybe by its repulsive smell, maybe by its ephemeral presence on the side of the road, can disrupt habits and precipitate new sensations and perceptions.

This movement of the senses and perception signals the terrain of micropolitics. It reminds us that this is where new techniques and capacities could emerge that change how we relate to ourselves and waste. For philosophers Michel Foucault and Gilles Deleuze ethics revolve around embodied practices and micropolitics of the self. They are grounded in actions and bodies rather than transcendent moral codes, and this incessant activity foregrounds the perpetual instability and ambiguity of norms, morality, and identity. Ethics are fundamental to the multiple processes of subjectification; they allow us to cultivate and organize ourselves not simply in relation to wider rules and moral interdictions but also in relation to "askesis," or cultivated sensibilities that establish the range of possibilities in perception, enactment, and responsiveness to others. Styles of waste disposal, then, are also styles of self; in managing waste we constitute an ethos and a sensibility. Our waste habits—all those repeated routines—leave their traces on our bodies and our environment.

The world of things and the pragmatic demands they make on us are central to the formation of an ethos. And with the rise of consumer cultures we have come to live with an enormous number of things. The scale of goods for sale and the amount of objects people accumulate have produced very distinct personal and domestic habits. Caring for the self has become complicated and intensified by the sheer density and diversity of possessions. While analyses of the social and economic impacts of consumption have been great for understanding the dynamics of exchange, circulation, and use, they have been less valuable for understanding our relations with the things we get rid of. For all the talk about how we occupy consumer culture there has been a cavalier disregard for the all wasted things that form an enormous part of this way of living. This book argues that it is crucial to make sense of the distinct ethos of waste that underpins consumption, to acknowledge that how we eliminate things is just as important as how we acquire them.

This does not mean that all our waste practices can be reduced to the cultural logic of consumer capitalism—person-thing relations are mediated by a multiplicity of forces. It simply means that commodity relations are one of the significant influences shaping habits of dispossession. And the general character of these waste habits is informed by relations marked by *distance, disposability*, and *denial*. Consumer cultures and the technocratic logics of efficiency and concealment have produced a distanced relation with wasted things even as amounts of waste have escalated phenomenally. External systems of removal from garbage trucks to sewers have dramatically reduced the demands waste makes on us. It simply gets taken "away," and while we know generally where it goes, the invisibility of these places, their location underground or on the margins of cities, facilitates denial or active not knowing. How exactly do the habits that distance us from wasted things become implicated in particular forms of embodiment? What sort of self do these habits shape? And in what ways could an ethos of distance, denial, and disposability be challenged?

I pursue these questions in the following chapters. The answers I develop come from close analyses of a series of strange encounters with waste. What unites these analyses is a desire to think about how unexpected experiences of waste can disrupt habits and trigger new relations and perceptions. My perceptions of waste, what it is, and what we do with it have been challenged by the examples I explore in this book. Sure, I was on the lookout for waste examples, but their impacts could not have been predicted. In trying to make sense of my responses to various wasted things, from the dancing plastic bag in *American Beauty* to thousands of perfectly rinsed and flattened milk cartons in a recycling depot in Kasaoka in Japan, I have drawn on a diverse set of conceptual and methodological tools. While some might find this heterogeneity unsettling or messy, the examples of waste explored here demanded it. This heterogeneity is a powerful reminder of the range of questions that waste provokes.

Poststructuralist political theory has been immensely important for helping me think through the relations between ethics and affect, and how our waste habits might be changed without recourse to guilt or moral righteousness. I use it in chapter 2, "Plastic Bags," to compare affective responses to waste (from disgust to enchantment) with the moral rhetoric of a recycling education program. In chapter 3, "Shit," the history of the sewer and Foucault's concept of biopower provide important tools for examining how our bodily waste mediates the public-private distinction and produces distinct forms of embodiment. I then analyze how waste becomes a political object. Using the examples of Bondi Beach's famous POOO Parades and the toilet festivals in the slums of Mumbai, I explore how privacy is publicly constituted and how a changed ethics of waste might involve new meanings for the intimate self. Chapter 4, "A Dumped Car," looks at person-thing relations using the practices of gleaning and making do. Through the example of two remarkable documentaries about different ways of living with waste, this chapter pursues the question of what might make us notice wasted things and invent different ways of living with them. My analysis draws on recent work in studies of material culture and thing theory to investigate how waste's materiality might become present to us. In chapter 5, "Empty Bottles," the rise of recycling is the focus. I look at recycling as a distinct cultural economy that has "enterprised" both waste and subjects. The creation of a new set of socio-technical relations around empty bottles and newspapers involves new habits and bodily performances, new calculations of value, and new discourses about the environment. Finally, in a chapter called "Worms," the idea of transience is examined through the example of the humble earthworm. What worms and their endless labor breaking things down show is how biological functions can have ethical resonance. In facilitating the transition from decay to renewal, worms display an exemplary relation to loss: they show how waste can be generative. How might we adapt the earthworm's arts of transience to our own lives? How might we live in a less destructive relation with waste and loss?

So it is on various durable practices and experiments in living with waste that I want to focus in this book, small everyday gestures rather than big political campaigns. This is not to abandon environmental politics but to come at it from a different angle, to ask different questions about configurations of "the political" and to use different tools.

I want to take seriously what it means to "act locally," and this means opening up a pathway from politics to ethics that makes it possible to consider the place of minor actions and tactics in living with waste. I want to examine the ideas and beliefs that shape social behaviors around waste and how they operate as a kind of second nature, an internalized, embodied set of dispositions that organize practices in certain unconscious ways. This should make it possible to give putting out the garbage the attention it deserves as a habit and, potentially, an ethic.

NOTES

1. Mary Douglas, *Purity and Danger* (London: Routledge & Kegan Paul, 1966).

2. Douglas, *Purity and Danger*, 35.

3. Brian Massumi, *Parables for the Virtual* (Durham, NC: Duke, 2002), 9 (emphasis in the original). Massumi's argument about the distinction between social determination and sociality is especially relevant here. Sociality demands a focus on the relational, or the processes of formation in which the social is determined.

4. The work of Julia Kristeva is crucial here, specifically *Powers of Horror* (New York: Columbia University Press, 1982).

5. Michel Foucault, *The Use of Pleasure*, trans R. Hurley (New York: Vintage, 1990), 25–26.

6. Bill Brown, *A Sense of Things* (Chicago: University of Chicago Press, 2003), 54.

7. *Active experimentation* is a term Gilles Deleuze and Claire Parnet use in their discussion of "Many Politics" in *Dialogues 11*, trans H. Tomlinson and B. Habberjam (London: Continuum, 1987), 137.

8. Paul Patton, *Deleuze and the Political* (London: Routledge, 2000), 7.

9. I take my lead from poststructuralist political theorists like Michel Foucault, Jane Bennett, Moira Gatens, Rosalyn Diprose, Paul Patton, William Connolly, and Gilles Deleuze, who all, albeit in different ways, investigate the political as a dynamic field of practices with the potential to contest dominant codes rather than a repressive hierarchy of social domination.

10. William Connolly, *Why I Am Not a Secularist* (Minneapolis: University of Minnesota Press, 1999), 176.

11. Fredric Jameson, *The Seeds of Time* (New York: Columbia University Press, 1994), xii.

12. The term *disenchantment stories* comes from Jane Bennett, *The Enchantment of Modern Life* (Princeton, NJ: Princeton University Press, 2001).

13. Bennett, *Enchantment*, 9.

14. This is Moira Gatens's argument in *Imaginary Bodies: Ethics, Power and Corporeality* (London: Routledge, 1996), viii.

15. Bruno Latour, *We Have Never Been Modern* (Cambridge, MA: Harvard University Press, 1993), 10–12.

16. Thanks to Simone Fullagar for this important point.

17. Brown, *A Sense of Things*, 18.

18. Pierre Bourdieu, *The Logic of Practice* (Stanford, CA: Stanford University Press, 1990), 59.

2

Plastic Bags

There is a scene in the popular Hollywood film *American Beauty* that prompted a wholly unexpected sadness in me. I'll call it the "rubbish scene": an extended video image of a plastic shopping bag blowing around in a strong wind. Everyone I have spoken to about this film remembers this scene, but they generally don't describe it as "sad"; beautiful, yes, moving and profound, no. Yet, for me, this scene was haunted. As alive as the bag was, as lyrical as its dance with the wind was, it was still a *plastic bag*. It could not entirely escape its materiality or its semiotics. The bag seemed to carry the whole enormous weight of ecological crisis. The lightness of the bag was in contrast with its burden as the penultimate sign of environmental catastrophe: a world drowning in plastic bags. A world in which we are constantly instructed to "say no to plastic bags!" The aesthetic resonances and animation could not completely override the moral undertones. The bag was rendered beautiful but this didn't make it good.

I have no doubt that this response was partially an effect of being rendered "environmentally aware"—all those years of public campaigns instructing me to resist the easy convenience of plastic bags and do my bit for nature. This training does not mean that I have completely eliminated plastic bags from my life, but it has meant that my relations with them have become more complicated. Perhaps this is why the redemptive gesture that structures the rubbish scene was so troubling. For redemption here meant the absolutely worthless and trivial transformed into the absolutely beautiful; redemption without any concern for moral or ecological consequences. I am simply too ambivalent about plastic bags for this transformation to be completely successful. For me the bag signified much more than the beauty of ephemera; it signified a major environmental problem rendered sensuous and enchanted. This scene invited me to change my feelings about plastic bags, to delight in something I have been trained to hate. I think this could be why I found it so deeply unsettling. I think this could be why I felt sympathy for the bag.

Consider another image of plastic bags, this time a television commercial made by the New South Wales Environmental Protection Authority (EPA). Here we see a man washing his car on the street without any concern for the gallons of soapy water draining into the storm water system. The next scene cuts to the interior of the drain, where we see the soapy water gushing on its way accompanied by street detritus. The final scene returns to the man, no longer cleaning the car but at leisure, swimming in a pristine river surrounded by bush, an image of Eden. He dives underwater and surfaces with a plastic bag clinging to his shoulder. With a shudder of aversion he flicks it off. Trust waste to spoil everything!

Unlike *American Beauty* the EPA allows for no ambiguity about the status of the bag. It is unequivocally bad. It is matter out of place, contaminating the purity of the natural with its sticky persistence. There is only one response to this bag, disgust. The bag disrupts the binary between pure and contaminated and in the same moment reminds us that binaries are more often than not unequal relations. For in this ad contamination is not simply purity's other, it is the lesser and devalued term in a moral framework.

Feeling moved by a plastic bag, feeling disgusted with a plastic bag: such different experiences of rubbish, such different relations with it. In *American Beauty* the bag is aestheticized and we are invited to see it as beautiful and enchanted. In the EPA ad the bag is an object of moral condemnation, an object that provokes judgment and guilt. It's not often that we experience rubbish as beautiful, and I am sure some would find this aestheticization of a major environmental problem grotesque. Yet, in this cinematic moment, the prescriptive logic of the EPA's waste education campaign is profoundly disturbed. For the *American Beauty* scene alludes to different ways of living with bags: to our various uses and experiences of them. It locates plastic bags in the realm of the sensual and the affective. And it refuses the essentializing move in much moral judgment that renders rubbish always already bad, thereby denying paradox and ambiguity—let alone any recognition of our shifting relational sensibilities with it.

Apart from startling me with its lyricism, what the scene in *American Beauty* did was remind me of the complex social life of bags. For much of their biography bags are very useful. They help us get the shopping home and then they store the rubbish that lots of the shopping becomes, they're great for putting wet swimsuits in at school, they are excellent for dust proofing. Often I feel gratitude for the humble practicality of a plastic bag: "Here, put it in a plastic bag." My point is not to defend plastic bags, to make a plea for a much-maligned object. It is simply to acknowledge the variety of relations we have with them in order to show that their status as rubbish is not fixed. That may be one of their identities, but it's not the only one. And it is this very ambiguity and complexity of uses that complicates moral rulings about and condemnations of bags as bad. For when you think about the particularity of bags in everyday life it is possible to see how changing habits and uses produce changing attitudes and modes of relating.[1] Sometimes bags are handy containers, at other times they are rubbish clogging up the kitchen drawer and making you feel guilty about their ultimate destination in a landfill. These shifts in everyday conducts and experiential networks of obligation are the stuff of ethics—not objects or practices classified as good or bad but relations of thinking, feeling, and acting.

My paradoxical reaction to these two images of rubbish is the impetus for this chapter. How is it that a scene from a hit movie has more emotional and political impact on me than an official waste education campaign? Why is it that the EPA campaign leaves me feeling guilty and patronized, irritated by its moralism and explicit pedagogical intent? Could it possibly be more "environmentally friendly" to feel sympathy and ethical concern for rubbish rather than disgust and anxiety about its destructive impacts on nature? How can these reactions and questions help develop an understanding of the place of waste in our ethical lives?

My aim is to open up other ways of thinking about the social regulation of everyday waste practices beyond command moralities: don't litter, refuse plastic bags, reuse and recycle. For as much as we may agree with such interdictions and recognize their rationality, cultivating such practices in our daily lives involves complex relations with both waste and our multilayered subjectivity.

Using some examples from waste education I want to examine the limits of social reform strategies that appeal to conscience, guilt, and obligation. The problem with these strategies is that, in the address to moral reason, bodily sensibilities and feelings are too often ignored. Rather than invoke morality, which can easily slide into moralism, it may be more effective to focus on questions of ethics and affect—to explore the terrain described by William Connolly as "that tropical undergrowth of life flourishing beneath the brittle trees of grand moral theory."[2] Here, Connolly argues, we confront the ubiquity of ethical work and its imbrication with the corporeal, its fundamental engagement with the most visceral registers of being.[3]

I begin with a brief exploration of how we learn the habit of wastefulness. In the previous chapter I suggest that disposability, distance, and denial best describe the ethos of waste in consumer culture. What forces prompted the cultivation of such waste habits? What sorts of changes to person-thing relations were necessary to facilitate the rise of disposability? I then consider how these waste habits have been morally problematized. The rise of public campaigns from antilitter to recycling depended on the presence of a conscience about rubbish: How was this conscience created? By investigating the links between conscience and forms of rule it is possible to see how state-driven waste education campaigns seek to change habits and reform conduct. It is also possible to see the limits of these strategies. Finally, I look at the relations between ethics and affect to see how waste habits might be changed without recourse to moral righteousness or resentment. Rather than seeking to master waste in the name of self-discipline and virtue, what would it mean to respond to it, to acknowledge our interconnections with it? Could our most visceral responses to waste be a source of new ethical practices?

LEARNING TO WASTE: THE ETHOS OF DISPOSABILITY

We need to get rid of things. Waste is something we all have to manage; beyond biological necessity we expel and discard in the interest of *ordering* the self, in the interest of maintaining a boundary between what is connected to the self and what isn't. Waste management in all its historical variety is fundamental to the practice of subjectivity. Styles of garbage elimination, then, can be located within Foucault's "arts of existence": all those actions and rules of conduct through which we organize ourselves according to particular ethical and aesthetic criteria.[4]

The arts of existence also involve habits. Habits locate us not simply in a social context but in a habitat, a specific place of dwelling or position. Our interactions with that place—what we make of it, what it makes of us—generate
a mode of being or ethos that structures social behavior, often below the
threshold of conscious decision making. Rosalyn Diprose reminds us that the
Greek word *ethos*, defined as character *and* dwelling, gives dwelling a double
meaning as both noun and verb, place and practice.[5] And from this notion of
dwelling as both habitat and habitual way of life the idea of ethics was derived.

> These habits are not given: they are constituted through the repetition of bod-
> ily acts the character of which are governed by the habitat I occupy. From this
> understanding of ethos, *ethics can be defined as the study and practice of that*
> *which constitutes one's habitat,* or as the problematic of the constitution of one's
> embodied place in the world.[6]

For Diprose ethics are not about universal principles and transcendent
moral positions. They are about modes of being in the world, or the relations
between being and the world; this grounds ethics in a constitutive relation between one's habitat and embodied character, or ethos. But it is not only habitat that is implicated in embodiment, it is also relations with others. These
force us to take a position, to establish an identity in and through relations of
differentiation with others. And, if the recognition of difference from others is
implicated in the constitution of an ethos and identity, so too is the recognition of difference from objects. Through habits we manage the circulation of
objects into and out of our lives and reestablish the boundaries of the self, and
this is how the cultivation of particular habits of waste removal becomes the
cultivation of a particular self.

In consumer cultures everyday waste habits express an ethos of disposability. What ethical criteria do these habits deploy, and what kind of self do they
make? How did disposability come to be seen as good? In her history of rubbish, *Waste and Want*, Susan Strasser gives some answers to these questions.
She challenges the assumption that the ethos of disposability is emblematic of
1950s consumerism.[7] For her, efficiency, cleanliness, and replaceability have
been a significant part of modernist culture since the days of paper collars in
the 1860s. The invention of a range of other disposable paper products took
off during the latter half of the nineteenth century, when paper became
cheaper and more readily available. By the early twentieth century paper cups

and straws were being introduced in the American railway system, the use of toilet paper was widespread in cities, and paper sanitary napkins were gaining acceptance. The appeal of disposable things was dependent on an accompanying discourse about disease and contamination. The rise of packaging, for example, was justified on the grounds that the consumer could be assured that the products were uncontaminated. As the idea of the "invisible germ" began to gain widespread popular attention the modern hygienic imagination grew, fuelling the take-up of these products. As Strasser says, "Comfort and morality united with science as the public learned that dirt and dust carried tiny creatures that caused illness."[8]

But there was also resistance to the rise of disposable products and the ethos of single use. Some people balked at having to pay for paper cups in coin-operated dispensers, others had always brought their own utensils when traveling, then there were those who were not convinced of the germ theory of disease. The modernist principle of purification that disposable products expressed was met with anger and incredulity in some quarters. Many people were hostile to the changes in relations with things that the disposable product inaugurated. They saw it as inefficient and wasteful and a challenge to a widespread ethos of thrift and reuse.[9]

Despite this resistance disposable objects spread as part of the general expansion of consumer culture. By the early 1920s another concept had emerged to justify their use: convenience. Economic rhetoric about efficiency and streamlined production began filtering into the home. This rhetoric was used to promote things like "labor saving" devices, packaged foods, washing powder, and the like—all in the name of freeing the housewife from drudgery and turning the household into a site of fast, competent production. Objects marketed as convenient or disposable evoked a modernist asceticism and temporality in which the technical was valorized for saving time and for its instrumental rationality.[10] Disposable things, like technology, satisfied needs fast and effectively. They helped to make housewives more efficient and to identify the truly modern household; they became markers of social distinction.

Ideas about purification and convenience were central to the promotion of disposable objects. These ideas helped people to develop ethical justifications for the particular habits that the disposable object demanded. They provided the wider discursive context whereby throwing things away came to be seen as both acceptable and normal. While there was a counterdiscourse about disposability as wasteful and a threat to more careful material relations, these negative connotations were marginalized as throw-away things spread and became incorporated into practices of the modern self and household management.[11] Using disposable things was an indicator of one's commitment to new standards of cleanliness and efficiency. These objects conferred status on the user.

But the most significant force fuelling the emergent ethos of disposability was the expansion of industrialization and the growth of mass consumption. This long and profound shift in the organization of economy and experience has been a central focus of modern social theory. My interest is in the logic of the commodity form and its impacts on waste habits. Commodity relations inaugurated major transformations in the structure of identity and the material everyday—the number of possessions people lived with, how they acquired them, and how they disposed of them.

Until recently, most accounts of how we occupy consumer culture have ignored the question of disposal. Yet it is impossible to understand the meanings of consumption as distinct practices of possession and accumulation without thinking about how these practices impact on *dis*possession. When the waste practices of consumer cultures are analyzed the tendency is to establish a crude causal relation between excess consumption and excess waste: easy come, easy go. While there is no doubt that the massive growth of consumption is directly linked to the massive growth of waste, this isn't much help in thinking about *how* consumption has changed waste habits; in understanding what this activity has done to the way we relate to things and the way we reject them.[12]

What is it about the structure of the commodity form that makes continual replacement both necessary and possible? Seriality and the fetish of the new provide key insights into this question. Constant change is fundamental to the expansion of markets and the circulation of the commodity form. The repetition of the ever new as ever the same, manifest in the fashion system and rapid turnover in style, shortens the life of the commodity and infuses person-thing relations with the logic of instant gratification. Commodity relations create a distinct temporality of desire that can be described as "never present to the object but always future or past."[13] In other words, the pleasure of a purchase is always fleeting; the satisfaction of desire that the commodity promises is never complete.

This distinct temporality of desire is linked to the fetish qualities of the com-modity. When commodities appear to us as fantastic, animated things with a life of their own it is easy to see why they are so enchanting. These changes in how objects are apprehended are not simply psychological, they are connected to the profound institutional changes that rapidly developing consumer cul-ture inaugurated. Bill Brown describes how the development of the depart-ment store created a theatricalized world of goods designed to inculcate desire. Fixed prices removed any need for the human interaction of bargaining and re-stricted consumption to a relation between consumer and merchandise. In this context objects' sensuous appeal was dramatically heightened.[14] The rise of ad-vertising was equally crucial in nurturing a fascination with the commodity and in normalizing the practice of shopping.

The general consensus in left critiques of mass consumption is that it has led to lives saturated with objects. However, within this material density the capacity to engage with the qualitative character of these objects has dimin-ished. This is because, when use value was replaced by exchange value, people no longer made the objects they lived with. They were distanced from the ob-jects' production and immediate materiality. German social theorist Georg Simmel describes this as the dialectic of proximity and distance, Marx as es-trangement and alienation.[15] Both are analyzing the process whereby, despite being surrounded by commodities, we are distanced from the material sub-stance of things. According to Marx, the damage of the commodity form is primarily felt in humans who are deprived of sensuous relations with things and succumb, instead, to crude fetish worship.

The problem with this account, as so many commentators have argued, is that it presumes a true or proper subject-object relation that capital and the rise of the commodity have destroyed. Taken to its logical extremes this cri-tique would have us all weaving our own clothes in a return to preindustrial authenticity. While the idea of alienation is not much help for challenging the ethos of disposability, it does describe an important aspect of how objects ap-pear to us in a commodity culture. The processes of alienation and abstrac-tion objectify both people and things. They substitute the qualitative for the quantitative and mask the unequal power relations that structure how com-modities are produced. This "phantom objectivity," as Marx calls it, is also the source of the commodity's fetish qualities, its capacity to seem animated and alive.

These complex processes of objectification and abstraction are at the heart of an ethos of disposability. They shape how we come to desire and accumulate commodities and how we come to reject them. Because we have little idea how commodities come into being, their life after we've finished with them, after their wondrous fetish qualities have petered out, is also of little or no interest. The magical qualities of the commodity obliterate its origin *and* its final destination. Often this destination may not be landfill; things can move out of commodity status without becoming rubbish. They might begin a life of lonely isolation in the shed or be born again into the gift economy of the charity shop. Chucking away is only one option, but it is an option made easier by the logics of fetishism and abstraction, which distance us from the life of commodities before and after they enter our lives: just get another one!

Single-use objects and commodities reconstituted person-thing relations in different, but related, ways. Both contributed to the rise of an ethos of disposability and the emergence of new waste habits that made throwing things away with little concern possible. Strasser is right in arguing that these changed relations with things had to be acquired and cultivated. But she is somewhat glib in reading these new relations as symptomatic of a "way of life remote from hand production."[16] This analysis reiterates all the problems of the alienation thesis, with its implicit refusal of the commodity and a yearning for more direct and transparent relations with objects.

This is not my argument. Rather, I am interested in how the ethos of disposability constituted waste as *ethically* insignificant. The kind of self produced through the habit of disposability was a self for whom "waste" had few moral connotations, a self whose waste practices confirmed its sense of mastery over and separation from the world. When commodity cultures redefined the meaning of freedom as "freedom to consume," this also meant freedom to waste. This didn't mean that disposability wasn't problematized in the expansion of commodity culture. Rather, it meant that the terms of this problematization did not involve reflective modification of the self. Before the emergence of environmentalism, the ethos of disposability framed waste as a *technical* rather than a *moral* problem, something to be administered by the most efficient and rational technologies of removal. Generally this meant (and continues to mean) dumping; the trash bin, the local dump, and the drain have become emblematic sites for the disposal of anything and everything; these are the homes of waste.

Yet, as anyone who has stood at the edge of a garbage dump or stared down a drain and felt a wave of horror and fascination would know, disposability is a technical and spatial fantasy. Our relations with waste cannot be so easily severed, out of sight does not necessarily mean out of mind. Disposability frames waste habits in terms of straightforward elimination, a necessary part of progress and consumption. This is a relation of mastery that constitutes the self that discards as separate and purified. And in this relation the ethical implications of our complex and shifting connections with rubbish are denied.

LEARNING NOT TO WASTE: BAD HABITS

It's harder to sell disposability now, perhaps because we've all seen too much rubbish. Waste has become visible, a landscape in its own right. This doesn't mean that disposing isn't flourishing; rather, a different problematization of waste has emerged over the last thirty years that has made trouble for the habit of thoughtless elimination. Technocratic discourses about efficient removal have been challenged by arguments about the moral and environmental effects of waste.

The antilitter campaigns that began in the late 1960s represented rubbish not just as matter out of place but also as morally unsettling, evidence of the collapse of civic obligation.[17] These campaigns linked the individual body to the social body. A favored image in them was (and still is) the disembodied hand in the act of dropping rubbish. This gesture of separation was no longer a sign of individual purification but a sign of pollution. It was evidence of an undisciplined self, unable to regulate its actions in the interests of social and environmental order, a self with no sense of public responsibility. This is how antilitter campaigns problematized the ethos of disposability, by implicating it in environmental and moral decline. Waste was exceeding its limits, it was no longer contained in appropriate places but was everywhere; classificatory boundaries were collapsing. The condition of "the environment" was threatened by the presence of rubbish, and so too were civic values.

These early antilitter campaigns were part of a major shift away from the idea of disposal as straightforward elimination toward the idea of disposal as a process of careful management. Waste is now something to be *managed*. Disposal has become implicated in a morality less concerned with maintaining the purity of the subject and more concerned with protecting the purity of the environment and establishing the virtue of the careful "waste manager." To manage waste has meant a reorganization of our relations with rubbish and self. Witness, for example, the phenomenal transformations in domestic waste practices evident in the normalization of recycling, in the instilling of a collective sense of individual responsibility for sorting our rubbish.

In constituting waste as a domain of moral concern, as a field of personal responsibility and careful domestic disciplines, we can see how everyday conducts were problematized and subjected to questioning—and how they were made the target of moral reflection. And it is in the space of the home, in the field of "domestic waste education" and the massive range of campaigns geared at transforming populations' waste practices, that we can see how routines and habits are implicated in particular sorts of subjectivity. In managing our domestic waste according to new principles of self-scrutiny, we are making the self an object of reflection in and through our relations with waste.

Waste is now a field of activity structured by legislated and normative moralities, by disciplinary codes that order conduct in the interests of wider objectives: from reduction of landfill to global ecological survival. It is a domain in which we have come to experience a sense of duty and responsibility for protecting the purity and otherness of the environment. The emergence of a waste management discourse shows how moral problematization has functioned to justify a range of interdictions and self-disciplines that have changed how we dispose of things. This is a technology of governing, a way of guiding conduct whereby we can see the links between the broader political rationalities of waste policy and the microtechnologies of daily life; whereby we can see how permeable the boundaries are between the domestic, the voluntary, and the governmental.[18]

And one effect of this is that putting out the garbage has become complicated. No longer the lugging of the bin to the curb a couple of times a week, now it's a complex assemblage of actions: collecting all the papers and cardboard (clean only) and putting them in their special container, rinsing the bottles and cans, removing labels and lids and allocating them to their container, putting the food scraps in the compost or worm farm (no meat), wheeling out the bin for everything else. These practices indicate the impacts of domestic waste education and the ways this has become enfolded with a new conscience about rubbish. And this conscience is a significant element of our attachment to changed waste habits.

There is no question that the demand to manage and minimize waste has come from coercive state programs and structural transformations in domestic waste services. But the success of these changes, in terms of widespread participation across populations, has depended on changes in the micropractices of everyday life, on the ways we've willingly acted on ourselves. This alignment of subjectivity with subjection is governance. But what is so significant about new rubbish habits is that, when questioned, many people claim they are doing it for nature not for the state. They are participating because they believe in some abstracted sense of social and environmental good. They experience recycling and composting as autonomous gestures, as expressions of their "environmentally concerned" identity.[19]

CONSCIENCE AND WASTE EDUCATION

What then is the logic of waste education, and how is it implicated in the idea of conscience and new forms of subjectivity? To answer this question I want to consider one example, the New South Wales Waste Service's "Are You a Good Sort?" campaign. The pun on "good sort" reveals how much our relations with waste have become reordered around a variety of new classificatory procedures, the assemblage of actions these demand, and the *virtue* that is attached to these. We can see here how abstract notions of care and management of the planet are linked to micropractices in the home, to instructions on how we should *be* around our rubbish: much more attentive, much more dutiful, much more careful than the culture of disposability, as careless disregard, ever demanded.

In the "Are You a Good Sort?" campaign sorting waste means regulating and disciplining personal practices in order to render the self more congruent with particular values like restraint ("Our beautiful city is running out of landfill areas so it's up to all of us to do our bit to help reduce the amount of garbage we throw out"); responsibility ("When shopping take your own shopping bag. Look for products in packs that can be refilled or recycled, and buy products made from recycled materials"); and economy ("All our waste management centers take recyclable materials for free so save yourself and your community a load of cash"). [20]

The macropolitical demand of waste policy, "Let's reduce waste," is successful only when, borrowing from Connolly, "micropolitical receptivity to it has been nurtured across several registers and constituencies."[21] But exactly which registers of being are addressed in the "Good Sort" campaign, and which are ignored or denied? In the appeal to restraint, responsibility, and economy, moral reason and judgment are privileged. The play of guilt and obligation are an ever-present subtext as we are extolled to do our bit. This is moral compunction. Obedience to new regimes of domestic waste management depend on a monitoring and disciplining relation to the self. And this relation is successful because it mobilizes conscience, because the rituals and habits of waste management have become implicated in reflexive techniques of the self.

Conscience is a potent reminder of how we make the self into an object of ethical attention; how we problematize and modify our conduct on the basis of ethical principles we aspire to. This particular relation to the self has a history. As Foucault has shown, conscience is a product of a range of techniques of the self that have come to constitute certain forms of personhood. To be a person now means cultivating particular modes of reflexivity. It means developing special ethical techniques and capacities, or "techniques of conscience."[22] These techniques and capacities are historically variable in their form and targets. Their presence is evidence not of a foundational interiority grounding the subject, but of shifting modes of living and self-cultivation. Human abilities can be ordered and understood without recourse to introspective moral problematization.[23]

Post-Foucauldian accounts of subjectivity reject metapsychology and its presumption of fundamental laws of interiority. Interiority is not a psychological system, nor is it the core of being. It is, according to Deleuze, a historically contingent discontinuous surface.[24] In the final two volumes of *The History of Sexuality* Foucault subjects interiority to radical critique. He investigates how relations to oneself and to others constitute subjectivity and how principles of internal self-regulation change. A central concern in this work is what happens when formerly esoteric ethical and spiritual practices are taken up by large-scale institutions such as the church and then bureaucratic states. This is the terrain of the government-subjectivity relation, in which relations to oneself become implicated in larger agencies of social regulation and power. When, according to Deleuze, "the individual is coded or recoded within a 'moral' knowledge . . . above all he becomes the stake in a power struggle."[25] This is the point when subjectivation becomes subjection, when power in the form of control and discipline becomes implicated in daily life and interiority. It is the point when subjects become tied to an identity by conscience and other techniques of moral self-knowledge and regulation. This is the point when we become guilty.[26]

The "Good Sort" campaign shows how processes of self-regulation and conscience shape our relations with waste, how circuits of guilt, self-reproach, and virtue have become enfolded with our intimate acts of disposing. The problem is that the "Good Sort" campaign's representations of rubbish practices deny other ways of being with waste. Waste habits are represented as flat, static, and mechanical, and easily altered with appeals to reason and conscience. There is no room for disgust or horror or pleasure or resentment. No room for movement between different registers of subjectivity or for any recognition of how changes in practices of the self may affect other ethical sensibilities. This type of moral instruction forecloses any possibility of understanding shifting forms of being in our relations with waste. Rubbish relations still mean mastery and control; we may have become more careful and attentive with our waste, but it is still absolutely and unquestionably separate from the self, something to be gotten rid of. Recycling and other new waste habits could be described as *virtue*-added disposal.

Unacknowledged in the "Good Sort" campaign are the implications such practices may have for our ethical and affective sensibilities around waste. Yet, in the demand to handle and sort our waste responsibly and to make aspects of it visible on the street, prior and entrenched senses of order and self-cultivation may well be unsettled. A letter to the editor of a local newspaper about hating recycling captures this tension beautifully:

> While in favor of recycling, the new, excessively complicated arrangements fail to cater to the needs of households in the following ways. The provision of four garbage receptacles is an eyesore and results in problems of storing these receptacles close to the street as well as out of direct vision. They are a major cause of visual pollution and convey a Third World appearance with garbage bins lining our streets. . . . These decisions are not in ratepayers' interests, despite the noble ideals which were possibly behind them.[27]

There is no doubt that this writer is uncomfortable with recycling. Stuff "noble ideals"; it's messy, offensive, and primitive. Beyond irritation there is the sense in which the disciplines of recycling contest the stability of the self.

They make trouble for existing forms of self-artistry and cultivation not simply through the privileging of a "third world" aesthetic but also through the affront to deeper and more visceral registers of being. The letter goes on to describe the sense of loathing and disgust experienced when rubbish sticks to the bottom of the bin as a result of constant compaction by householders desperate to make all their waste fit in the new half-size containers. Then there are the effects of dogs and wind disturbing overfull bins. Being aware of the moral pressure to recycle does nothing to lessen the horror of it all because, for this writer, judgment is a product of much more than rational argument.

Unlike the "Good Sort" campaign this letter gets to the heart of waste's relationality. Having to manage waste under this new regime disturbs identity. If waste is one of our most immediate others, and establishing our difference and separation from it the condition of possibility for a self, then its persistence, its refusal to go, is a primordial threat to the drive for wholeness. The self exists only in relation, but rubbish practices based on expulsion and elimination maintain the fantasy of separation and sovereignty. New waste habits disrupt this. Not only do we have to handle our waste much more, it sticks around longer and aspects of it become public. The implications of this for this letter writer are more than guilt and resentment about an imposed moral duty; they are about the ethical effects of recycling practices on habits and sensibilities. They are about the unsettling impacts of recycling on the micropolitics of the self. They are about encounters he doesn't want to have.

The implied references to aesthetics and abjection in this response to recycling reveal the heterodox nature of ethics and their relative autonomy from wider social and governmental regulations. This letter describes an experience of ethical discontent that emerges from a waste ethos constituted around *aesthetic* rather than environmental values. For the aggrieved letter writer the rules and domestic disciplines that recycling programs demand harbor no opportunities for artistic practice.[28] In fact, they disrupt the relations between order and beauty, aesthetics and ethics that are fundamental to his arts of existence; hence his resentment. He can feel the pull of moral reason. He has a conscience about waste but he also has sensibilities, disciplined forms of sensuousness that are seriously offended by these practices. He isn't mourning the planet, he's mourning the pleasures of disposal free of macropolitical governmental restraints.

ETHICS AND AFFECT

If we accept that disposal is necessary, how could it be recast in ways that acknowledge the ethical significance of rubbish without generating moral righteousness or resentment? Domestic waste education campaigns seek to reorder conscience and habits around waste in certain ways. But this plane of macropolitical organization, as Deleuze and Guattari call it, exists in a relationship of tension and negotiation with other planes and dimensions of being.[29] Deleuze and Guattari's insistence on the plurivocity of being, on the multiplicity of dimensions, lines, and directions, signals how movements of becoming and immanence fragment the normative work of macropolitics. It also signals an ethics that has little to do with rule-bound moralities.

In his readings of Foucault and Spinoza Deleuze is concerned with forms of being that exist *beyond* or in the interstices of guilt and conscience. In seeking to restore ethics to explorations of ways of living and the molecular in-between of subjects, he privileges ethical practices that depend less on external authority, such as state disciplines and prescriptive moral codes, and more on cultivations and sensibilities. Deleuze's metaphor of the fold is central to this ethics. The fold presumes not simply a self in relation but also a self without any essential interiority. The inside is an enfolding of the outside; folds incorporate without totalizing, internalize without unifying; they make spaces, surfaces, flows, and layers. "Subjectivation is created by folding, by bending the outside through practical exercises."[30] And, Deleuze argues, even though Christian technologies of the self may have transformed the person into a site of subjection, subjectivation persists in those spaces and folds in which the relation to oneself resists being codified by agencies of power-knowledge: "The relation to oneself is continually reborn, elsewhere and otherwise."[31] Deleuze's use of resistance does not imply some essence of the self called *agency* or whatever. Rather, it signals sensibilities and intensities moving below and within those folds of the self that are implicated in modes of obligation to various forms of authority.

Deleuze's account of enfolding has been taken up by theorists of governmentality.[32] In seeking to understand the relation between the forms of truth in which being is problematized and the habits and practices through which we shape our own and others' conduct, this work effectively decenters notions of conscience, rule, and authority. It allows us to see how governing in all its permutations and variations is doubled, or implicated in modes of ethical reflection and practice. Yet, as useful as this work is for thinking about rule as a form of enfolding, it seems to involve a very partial and particular reading of Deleuze. Studies of government allow us to see how conscience is a mode of obligation to rules and norms, how the "fold of the relation between forces according to a particular rule" constitutes us as governable subjects.[33] What they are less able to see are those forces of ethical life and being—those encounters, visceral movements, and differences—that initiate *other* possibilities for subjectivity and intersubjectivity, or what Connolly calls the movements of becoming.

So it is to Connolly's rich and suggestive dialogue with Deleuze and Nietzsche, particularly in chapter 3 of *Why I Am Not a Secularist*, that I want to turn to in order to see how new ethical possibilities around waste might be initiated. For Connolly's question is not that of the governmentality theorists—how codes of morality and normativity are enfolded with particular habits of being. Rather, Connolly asks how new identities and ethical attachments can emerge out of the unexpected energies and disturbances that unsettle being. How does being operate in a paradoxical relation of tension and interdependence with the movements of becoming?[34] Connolly argues that conscience and other code-driven moral techniques are crude and blunt tools for coping with the world. Their tendency to ground moral actions in law, god, global survival, consensus, or any other categorical imperative makes them blind to the ambiguous and disturbing aspects of most ethical encounters. The moral weight of codes and doctrines turns obligation into duty, guilt, and resentment: "I *should* do this . . . because the environment is suffering, because I am law abiding, because I am virtuous." This is obligation working in the interests of mastery and self-certainty, obligation that undermines senses of ethical connection in order to maintain the stability of being. This is obligation as a moral technique that suppresses the visceral and the situational.

Yet, in the new experiences of obligation to our rubbish that recycling and composting have initiated, the visceral is ever present and palpable. We may act out of concern for the suffering of the environment, out of duty and guilt, but we are also touching and sorting that which has lost value, is rotting, and is in a state of irretrievable decay; we see the end of mastery, we see becoming. And our responses are shifting and surprising. The compost bin becomes a site of beauty and fecundity—all those worms, all that soil in the making. The spilled rubbish spread over the footpath after pickup gives you a shudder of aversion way beyond mere irritation. Why is that such a disturbing sight? These moments of intensity surprise and unsettle, they reveal a responsiveness to waste circulating through every dutiful and correct practice. And it is in these moments of responsiveness, these currents of movement and affect within the self, in the self's relation to otherness, that Connolly locates the politics of becoming.

Connolly's argument about responsiveness resonates with Deleuze and Guattari's idea of the body as a plane of affects: "Affects are becomings. . . . We know nothing about a body until we know what it can do, in other words, what its affects are, how they can enter into composition with other affects, with the affects of another body."[35] For Connolly, responsiveness is a condition of possibility, it opens up lines of mobility and difference within the self, and it is something that can be cultivated. An ethos of critical responsiveness connects becoming to various practices of self-modification. It involves work on the self in the interests of recognizing the plurivocity of being and denaturalizing identity as stasis or essence.[36]

What, then, would an ethos of critical responsiveness look like in relation to rubbish? Has it not already begun with the new waste regimes that we now practice? Yes and no. The moral problematization of waste has established new relations of obligation and duty with our rubbish, it has initiated different responses to it, but these still generally appeal to categorical moral imperatives: global ecological survival, the care of the planet. The regulatory disciplines involved often sit uneasily with other sensibilities and micropolitics of the self, as the letter on hating recycling shows. In other words, domestic waste education privileges a fairly restricted set of responses to waste, and these are inextricably linked to the constraints of moral codes, which too easily slide into moralism. Guilt, resentment, and anxiety are not politically productive. Sure, they may have mobilized people to change their habits, but they inhibit other responses and possibilities, other ways of being with waste. A politics of becoming does not proceed from guilt. It proceeds from a critical responsiveness, critical in the sense that those intensities and affects in the interstices of guilt and conscience awaken us to our own becoming.

So much waste education secures an obligation to new techniques and habits by insisting that the threat of waste be mastered: reduced, reused, recycled. This fantasy of control establishes the responsible self as separate from the world. It maintains an absolute alterity of waste and blinds us to an awareness of how our relations with it are fundamental to the very possibility of life. Mastery inhibits the possibility of seeing in waste our own unremitting unbecoming. But it is never complete or successful, as responses of unease or pleasure or grief reveal. And surely it is here, with these openings and intensities, that different ethical relations with waste could be established, that obligation could become responsiveness.

I can think of only a few waste education campaigns that presume a pleasure and generosity in waste: celebrations of composting and a campaign run by Brisbane City Council called "Enjoy Your Garbage." In composting campaigns organic waste is often represented as beautiful, its formless disorder reconstituted as an aesthetic of abundance; scraps, discards, leftovers becoming soil. Then there are slogans like "What you don't eat your garden will." The play here is on sameness, on the similarities between self and garden, on exchanges that connect. Composting is framed as a gift; in cultivating a sensibility for it we are cultivating a waste ethos that proceeds from generosity rather than guilt.

The "Enjoy Your Garbage" campaign was more ambiguous. It involved putting that slogan on garbage trucks, in all education materials to households, and in a series of radio ads. But behind all this was a pretty standard set of prescriptions about reducing, recycling, and composting. Enjoyment was to be found in doing the right thing, in self-discipline. Still, there is something unsettling and suggestive about the interdiction to *enjoy*. Is this the pleasure of control or of care and deliberation? Who can say? But at least enjoyment cultivates other responses and ways of being with waste beyond moral duty or disgust.

What this campaign does invoke is Italo Calvino's beautiful essay on putting out the garbage, *La Poubelle Agreee*, in which pleasure and enjoyment, not duty or disgust, are the central emotions. This essay is a series of reveries on rubbish rituals. In common with waste educators Calvino is concerned with practices, with our everyday behaviors around rubbish:

> Here I am, then, on my way downstairs already, holding the bucket by its semicircular handle, taking care it doesn't swing too much and spill its contents. The lid I usually leave behind in the kitchen: it's an irksome accessory, that lid, it never quite manages to combine its two tasks of concealing the rubbish and getting out of the way when you have to chuck more in. The compromise one

settles for involves keeping it at an angle, a bit like a mouth opening, trapping it between the bucket and the wall in precarious equilibrium. . . . That transfer from one container to another, which for most inhabitants of the metropolis takes on the significance of a passage from public to private, for me, in our house, in the garage where we keep the big poubelle during the day, is only the last gesture of the ceremonial upon which the private is founded.[37]

But unlike most waste education Calvino's story considers these practices in terms of their phenomenological and sacred resonances. The pleasure he gets from putting out the garbage is not the pleasure of being virtuous, of being a "good sort," it is the pleasure of habit and order. The gesture of throwing away is the "first and indispensable condition of being," for one is what one does not throw away. In the purifying ritual of putting out the rubbish we not only confirm who we are, the boundaries of the self, we also create the conditions for renewal. For Calvino every act of rubbish disposal is a little funeral that postpones our own inevitable demise, it is an offering "made to the underworld, to the gods of death and loss."[38]

What is so startling about Calvino's essay is the absence in it of guilt and resentment. He does not experience putting out the rubbish as coercion or moral duty, though he is aware of the municipal rules that structure his practices. For him, rubbish has other values and meanings; its disciplines, its rituals, awaken him to the pleasures of self-cultivation. Waste here is not something to be reduced, recycled, reused. He does not frame his relation to it through the discourses of environmental awareness. Rather, it is a fundamental component of the arts of existence, of the habits and sensibilities that give meaning and order to the self. It is an activity through which we are able to reflect on ways of being. Calvino's ethos of waste blurs the distinctions between thinking and feeling, putting out the garbage is both an intellectual and spiritual experience. Its effects reverberate through several registers of being. Through waste practices we sense the limits of the self and connect with wider forces. In enjoying waste, he is deriving pleasure from the careful management of loss and disposal.

In his reveries on rubbish, Calvino is open to the ways in which waste management alludes to other ways of being: the inevitably of death, the profound comfort of ritual, the sensuality and pleasure in maintaining order. Unlike the letter writer incensed about recycling Calvino has no anxiety about the boundaries between himself and his garbage. Instead of stinginess and irritation he expresses openness and generosity. Instead of a binary, a fixed opposition, he sees an active relation, a movement in which the identities of waste and the self are implicated in each other. This is an evocative account of relationality, of the liminal space in which separation meets connection. Calvino does not deny the necessity of disposal; putting out the garbage is a gesture of separation that prevents merger and contamination, but it is also, paradoxically, connection. It links him to wider experiences of loss and ritual. For separation is a relation, it is not the opposite of connection; to experience ourselves as separate from rubbish is still to be in a relation with it. This is the messiness and ambiguity that marks our relations with rubbish and exposes the fantasy of a pure and stable morality. And this is the messiness and ambiguity that makes ethical work experimental, creative, and relational.

These may seem weak, even pathetic, alternatives to the power and urgency of campaigns based on guilt and mastery. But much like the plastic bag scene in *American Beauty* they recognize a wider range of responses to rubbish than moralism ever does. They implicitly speak to our plurivocity of being; they acknowledge our dependence on waste, the ways in which we need it to maintain a bounded self; but they don't convert this dependence into resentment or fear. Connolly suggests that the most complex ethical issues arise in contexts in which intense suffering is implicated in securing the "self-confidence, wholeness, transcendence and cultural merit of others. That is, the most intense, intractable cases of suffering are political in character. They often revolve around . . . the politics of becoming."[39] There is no doubt that the environment, "nature," is suffering due to the burden of our excessive waste; that our sense of transcendence and mastery over nature emerges, in part, from our capacity to dump waste on it. As Michel Serres says, one of the ways in which we possess nature is by fouling it.[40] But in seeking to change this, politics driven by the logics of moral imperatives and guilt can go only so far. A politics of becoming proceeds from those responses to waste that unsettle mastery, those intensities that signal not our difference from waste but our profound implications with it.

NOTES

A version of this chapter was published as "Plastic Bags: Living with Rubbish" in the *International Journal of Cultural Studies* 4, no. 1 (2001).

1. See Steven Connor's account of the cultural phenomenology of bags in "Rough Magic: Bags" in *The Everyday Life Reader*, ed. Ben Highmore (London: Routledge, 2002).

2. William Connolly, *Why I Am Not a Secularist* (Minneapolis: University of Minnesota Press, 1999), 17.

3. Connolly, *Why I Am Not a Secularist*, 3.

4. Michel Foucault, *The Use of Pleasure*, trans. R. Hurley (New York: Vintage, 1985).

5. Rosalyn Diprose, *The Bodies of Women* (London: Routledge, 1994), 19.

6. Diprose, *Bodies of Women*, 19 (emphasis in the original).

7. Susan Strasser, *Waste and Want: A Social History of Trash* (New York: Metropolitan Books, 1999).

8. Strasser, *Waste and Want*, 174.

9. In chapter 5 I explore the nineteenth-century ethos of reuse and recycling in more detail.

10. See Thomas Tierney, *The Value of Convenience* (New York: State University of New York Press, 1993). Tierney argues that techno-fetishism is ultimately predicated on a fear and evasion of death and a desire to overcome the inconvenient body.

11. For a good discussion of the tensions between hygiene and thrift in the rise of disposability see Gavin Lucas, "Disposability and Dispossession in the Twentieth Century," *Journal of Material Culture* 7, no. 1 (2002).

12. In chapter 4 I look at some of the recent work being done in studies of material culture on waste practices.

13. Lucas, "Disposability," 17.

14. Bill Brown, *A Sense of Things* (Chicago: University of Chicago Press, 2003), 31.

15. Georg Simmel, *The Philosophy of Money* (London: Routledge, 1978); and Karl Marx, *Capital*, vol. 1. (Moscow: Progress, 1971).

16. Strasser, *Waste and Want*, 265.

17. See, for example, Dorothy Shuttlesworth, *Litter—The Ugly Enemy* (New York: Doubleday, 1973).

18. Mary Poovey, *Making a Social Body* (Chicago: University of Chicago Press, 1995), 12.

19. Of course there are plenty of people who experience new rubbish regulations as coercive and repressive, evidence of government desire to control aspects of private life. I consider an example of this later in this section.

20. "Are You a Good Sort?" leaflet, Sydney, New South Wales Waste Service, n.d.

21. Connolly, *Why*, 149.

22. Ian Hunter, "Subjectivity and Government," *Economy and Society* 22, no. 1 (1993): 128.

23. Hunter, "Subjectivity and Government," 128.

24. Gilles Deleuze, *Foucault*, trans. S. Hand (Minneapolis: University of Minnesota Press, 1995).

25. Deleuze, *Foucault*, 103.

26. Making sense of conscience has been a significant focus of post-Foucauldian accounts of the subject. Judith Butler's dialogue with Foucault in *The Psychic Life of Power* (California: Stanford University Press, 1997) is driven by the desire to think his theory of power together with a theory of the psyche. If interpellation is the moment when the subject is affected by subordination and normalization, the moment when we turn guiltily to the voice of the law, Butler argues, what is needed is an understanding of the psychic operations of regulatory norms, or a theory of conscience. Butler's account of interiority focuses on how norms and disciplines assume a psychic character, on the moments when a subject turns on itself and works in tandem with processes of social regulation. This process reveals the complex ways in which power is reiterated within the subject; the ways in which we become guilty.

27. Letter to the editor, *North Shore Times*, October 16, 1998.

28. See Jane Bennett, "How Is It, Then, That We Still Remain Barbarians?" *Political Theory* 24, no. 4 (1996), for an excellent discussion of the relationship between ethics and aesthetics in Foucault.

29. Gilles Deleuze and Felix Guattari, *A Thousand Plateaus: Capitalism and Schizophrenia*, trans. B. Massumi (London: Athlone, 1988), 33.

30. Deleuze, *Foucault*, 104.

31. Deleuze, *Foucault*, 104.

32. See, for example, Mitchell Dean, "Foucault, Government and the Enfolding of Authority," in *Foucault and Political Reason*, ed. A. Barry, T. Osborne, N. Rose (Chicago: University of Chicago Press, 1996).

33. Deleuze, *Foucault*, 104.

34. Connolly, *Why*, 195.

35. Deleuze and Guattari, *Thousand Plateaus*, 256–57.

36. Connolly, *Why*, 69.

37. Italo Calvino, "La Poubelle Agreee," in *The Road to San Giovanni* (London: Jonathon Cape, 1993), 96.

38. Calvino, "La Poubelle Agreee," 104.

39. Connolly, *Why*, 51.

40. Michel Serres, *The Natural Contract* (Ann Arbor: University of Michigan Press, 1995).

3

Shit

It's difficult to imagine a world without a distinction between public and private, though there are times when you get an insight into what it might be like. Seeing half the contents of your garbage bin spread over the street after collection night is one of those times. After irritation, this experience can trigger strong feelings of exposure. All this evidence of your intimate life is revealed as waste. In the rush to pick it up you shudder with the horror of contamination and embarrassment. When waste returns, your privacy is exposed to unwelcome scrutiny.

Consider a different example. After heavy rain Sydney's storm water system, designed to manage runoff from streets, is regularly polluted with raw sewage that leaks into it from broken pipes and an aging infrastructure. This makes the beaches dangerously toxic and it can produce a strange miasma. When the rain clears and everything is meant to smell fresh and cleansed, there is often a strong stench emanating from gutters and street grates. Shit is in the air. This is unpleasant in a crinkled nose, "What's that smell?" kind of way, but you generally don't feel personally implicated. You don't feel that your privacy has been challenged. It's an environmental problem, a failure of government. It can upset senses of civic order and public health, but our response is most often limited to "What are 'they' going to do about it?" if we even care at all.

In these two urban encounters waste mediates the public-private distinction in quite different ways. In the first, it is resolutely connected to practices of the personal, to rituals of everyday life and routines of self-maintenance. Waste functions as a marker of the structural differentiation between the realm of intimacy and public life. Managing it is something you do in private, something that is naturalized as part of a prepublic individuality. The removal of waste, while bureaucratically managed, takes place largely in secret. While our bottles and papers may be displayed on the street in recycling crates for all to see, our really intimate waste, the waste that has been closest to our bodies or that is organic, is secreted away in drains and enclosed bins. While the blocked or overflowing toilet may be the ultimate domestic nightmare, spilt trash cans can generate a similar sense of horror. Even though trash can waste is not shit, it can metonymically suggest it. Contact with its slimy, putrefying reality has the capacity to disturb the body's boundaries and sense of stability. Waste that is most threatening to the self has to be rendered out of sight as quickly as possible.

In the second encounter, the sight or smell of sewage in public can generate special investigative media reports and even the occasional beachside mass demonstration. Accounts of this waste management problem constitute it as a failure of the state. Using the rhetoric of environmentalism they are full of shocking statistics, attacks on utilities, and queries about threats to public health and ocean life. Sewage is represented as the domain of infrastructure; its unwelcome appearance on the shoreline or gushing out of storm water chan-nels straight into the ocean triggers all sorts of anxieties: possible epidemics, a site of pleasure and hedonism threatened, fear of a poisoned world.

The differences between these examples seem straightforward. There's pri-vate waste that is nobody's business but ours, and there's public waste that is the responsibility of government. The status of waste in public and private spheres seems incommensurable. When we manage waste at home our sub-jectivity and intimate self are at stake. When we protest about filthy beaches and ocean outfalls we become activist citizens concerned to make the state ac-count for its actions: concerned to advocate for oceans to be protected from gross exploitation and contamination.

The waste we manage at home in rituals of personal care seems resolutely different from the effluent that horrifies us spilling over into public space. In the long journey from the bathroom to the ocean, via underground networks of sewers and treatment works, our bodily waste is transformed and so too is our relationship to it. The infrastructural logic of sanitation is not just technical but cultural. Sewers function as a mediating system reordering the bio-logical effects of shit and also its political and social meanings. This means that when we protest about visible urban waste and ocean pollution our per-sonal waste practices are displaced by the performative demands of being a "concerned public." And in order for us to be a public, to invoke notions of "public" health or "public" interest or "public" outrage, a generalization and abstraction must take place. Michael Warner argues that publics involve the active suspension of selfhood, the denial of any sense of particular bodies with their messy biological processes: "The moment of apprehending something as public is one in which we imagine, if imperfectly, indifference to those partic-ularities, to ourselves."[1] In other words, publics don't shit.

I am both fascinated and troubled by this proposition. Fascinated because it signals the important place of waste in the formation of the modern sub-ject. Troubled because I wonder about the effects of this denial of the shitting body on activist campaigns around ocean pollution. Does this denial limit the political imagination of such campaigns? Does it restrict our sense of obliga-tion to the oceans and rivers where our waste ends up? In taking up Warner's challenge to understand how private life can be made publicly relevant, I want to investigate the relationship of our most intimate waste management prac-tices to public campaigns around shit. I want to think about the ethical and environmental implications of our attachment to particular waste habits. What do these habits mean for the self and its most visceral registers *and* for notions of civic order and environmental purity?

While different measures of cleanliness and purity operate in public and private, both spheres depend on efficient techniques of waste elimination to ensure that shit doesn't disturb the stability of system. When shit happens, the demand for it to be rendered invisible and odorless generally means disposal in a place classified as somehow outside both the public and the private—oceans and rivers, for example. The cultural and political distinctions between public and private are sustained by the gross exploitation of what is at once both "nature" and a secondary treatment facility.

My aim in this chapter is to understand how the problematization of shit in public is implicated in the "privatization" of shit. When human waste management was made a state matter through the formation of regulations and institutions to administer it, the realm of privacy and personal habit was substantially reordered. And it is only by understanding how shit has been deployed to produce a modern public and private distinction that it is possible to assess the fundamental paradox of shit in public. A paradox that goes something like this: horror at the very idea of defecating on the street and resigned acceptance of overflowing storm water drains and waste treatment facilities pouring raw sewage into the ocean.

But does the sight of shit overflowing its limits ever completely repress the fact of our private waste practices? Or are the forms of embodiment and the social relations that surround this most intimate waste matter too powerful to contain? And, if they are, in what ways could they be used to generate new campaigns against environmental disintegration, new practices of citizenship and everyday intimacy? In the second half of this chapter I look at two remarkable protests about shit: the POOO parades on Bondi beach in the late 1980s, at which thousands of Sydneysiders rallied against the polluting effects of an aging ocean outfall; and the ongoing toilet festivals of Mumbai, at which slum dwellers design and build their own toilets so they won't have to live with the health risks of shitting in public. As I outline in chapter 2, ethics are embodied, and they emerge out of experiential networks of obligation. What I am investigating here is how techniques to manage our biological waste either implicate us in or blind us to these networks of obligation. Does the management of shit—a process that is at once technological, governmental, intimate—energize our ethical imagination or numb it? In the protests analyzed here we can see how shit motivates people to public political action. But what are the impacts of these actions on ethical sensibilities and the meanings of privacy?

Warner argues that struggles over the meanings of sexual intimacy and privacy have the potential to elaborate different practices.[2] They can imagine different worlds that make trouble for oppressive public norms and restricted cultural contexts. Could the same be said of defecating? The visceral intensity of these struggles, their transgressive capacity to disrupt the boundaries that we take as "natural," is a stark reminder of the political power of disturbance. In experiences of horror and abjection we confront the constitutive uncertainty of naturalized cultural distinctions. There is no doubt that shit (like sex) can be very disturbing, and this is why it is of inestimable value for understanding the contingency of cultural boundaries.

By focusing on the politics of disturbance rather than the politics of shit I want to expand the focus of environmental accounts of human waste management.[3] These accounts often get bogged down in endless disputes over good and bad ways to eliminate shit, environmentally sound versus environmentally destructive. The politics of disturbance proceed from a quite different set of assumptions: the fundamental contingency of the cultural conventions and distinctions through which we order our bodies and world. Like Warner, I am interested in the active, creative *use* of transgression and disturbances in the formation of new political responses and new ethical sensibilities. This approach resonates with William Connolly's argument about the political force of disturbance: "The key may be to turn disturbance of what you are into a critical responsiveness of what you are not."[4] Disturbances, rather than enforcing a dogmatic reassertion of self or norms, could *expose* contingency and interdependency, thereby provoking different engagements with the world, different ways of living with shit.

HISTORIES OF SHIT

Revisiting the history of shit will set the scene—but not just any history of shit. The language of modern government and family contributed to the transmutation of shit, implicating it in the reordering of bodies, space, and urban administration. The task, here, is to track these transmutations and their role in differentiating public and private. Triumphalist accounts of engineering and civic improvement are not much use. Their ideologies of progress tend to cloud the issue.[5] While it is easy to reduce the history of sanitation to technological innovation and a few male visionaries, the effect is to write bodies and discourse out of the story. Yet the question is precisely the links between bodies, infrastructure, and social regulation.

The sewer may be a great technological achievement, but it is also what *literally* connects shit as public problem and shit as private secret. Sewers link us to the state without any sense of direct intervention. They are where citizenship and subjectivity intermingle. Their technical and hygienic effects cannot be isolated from their ethical and social ones. Flushing and washing your hands, rituals of cleaning and self-care, as naturalized as they seem, are a product of very particular forms of reason; habitus has a history. Rather than being the bottom line of the body's biological identity, shit, like sex, has been subject to shifting mentalities. This means that the biological reality of shit is less the object than our relationships with it: how practices of personal waste management are caught up in larger political assemblages and become implicated in the constitution of the self.

Foucault described this process whereby modern forms of rule work on the body as biopower.[6] He argued that biopower makes "life" into a political object, and that its effects operate through the creation of biological norms. The paradoxical issue with shit is whether it was seen as part of life or whether it was connected to death and decay. In the histories I review here the status of human waste is ambiguous. It is both something that needs to be managed efficiently in order to secure the integrity of natural phenomenon in populations; and something to be hidden away and rendered secret because of its connection to death—which, Foucault notes, is power's limit, the moment that evades it.

According to Foucault, biopower emerged as the dominant mechanism of state power in the nineteenth century. This was when the normalizing imperatives of various biopolitical technologies—from statistics on birth rates to sewers—reached into the vital fundamentals of human existence, shaping bodies in relation to biological norms. Biopower operates directly on bodies; it works not through the meditation of consciousness or through repressive force, but by implicating individuals in relations of identification and differentiation from norms.[7] The challenge in thinking about the history of shit, then, is to understand its biopolitical effects; to track how various changes in the way it was administered created new normalizing imperatives about its intimate management and its role in public order.

"Surely, the State is the Sewer"—this is how Dominique Laporte begins chapter 3 of his brilliantly scatalogical *History of Shit*.[8] It's an important claim and one that is endorsed by two other valuable accounts of the place of waste in modern social administration. Both Mary Poovey, in *Making a Social Body*, and Thomas Osborne, in his essay "Security and Vitality: Drains, Liberalism and Power in the Nineteenth Century," make the same point, albeit without the literary flourishes.[9] Reading these texts together is productive. All are attentive to how bodies became the literal sites for modern biopolitical norms, and all are concerned to track the shifting forces (discursive, economic, political) that made shit thinkable as a public problem and *un*thinkable as a private secret.

Poovey, Laporte, and Osborne examine the processes whereby shit became a political object and show how this constituted new norms for privacy and domesticity. In different ways they all echo Warner's key point that "privacy is publicly constructed."[10] But how did the state become the sewer? How did shit, or the "sanitary idea," become a major impetus for state formation? How did the problem of biological waste energize the state and help it consolidate its apparatuses and techniques?

Laporte's approach to these questions is unashamedly Lacanian.[11] He equates the state with the Law but this totalizing impulse is tempered by a historical method that is evocatively Foucauldian. He defines the relation between shit and power in terms of exclusion and repression. However, he is aware of the fact that repression is part of the same historical network as the thing it denounces. In this way *History of Shit* resonates with *The History of Sexuality* in that both describe the frenzy to put into discourse what is sentenced to disappear or classified as secret. For Laporte, Foucault's critique of the repressive hypothesis is equally applicable to shit. Rather than power imposing taboos of nonexistence and silence, it produces, brings into being, knowledges and technologies whose effect is not the prohibition but the organization of secrets. "We dare not speak about shit. But . . . no other subject—not even sex—has caused us to speak so much."[12]

Laporte begins his history with two sixteenth-century edicts. One was to clean up official language and enforce the compulsory use of maternal French; the other was to clean up the streets—to forbid the tossing of refuse out of windows because it was impeding the movements of trade. The policing of speech and an emergent politics of waste were linked by law and commerce. So Laporte establishes a relationship between purity, political authority, and capitalism. But this is no standard Marxist account of the rise of the state driven by the growing demands of capital accumulation. It is more an account of how the state acquires divine or celestial capacities, how it comes to be understood as inviolable and therefore capable of purifying the most repulsive things.[13] The constitution of money as dirty and corrupting was fundamental to the rise of the market economy. Separating unclean financial transactions from the realm of the state and relegating them to the private paralleled the privatization of waste; the demand that shit be removed from public gaze and dealt with in households:

> Thus, as a "private" thing—each subject's business, each proprietor's responsibility—shit becomes a political object through its constitution as the dialectical other of the "public." From the sixteenth century on, the State initiates a contradictory discourse on waste that is nonetheless consistent with its

definition of state capitalism: a discourse that urges proprietors to become even richer, while casting a withering eye on the foul odor of their accumulations.[14]

For Laporte it was commerce and shit that helped found the early modern state. This is not to deny the significance of language and territory but to make a case for the state as a purifying force that establishes its power through its capacity to remove filthy things to the category of the private. Shit had to be excluded from the official in order to establish the state's power to cleanse. But this exclusion did not involve the construction of sewers, the creation of an infrastructure for the subterranean management of threats to life. The focus of these sixteenth-century edicts was not the biological needs of individuals. The health of that abstract category "the population" was not the objective. This management of shit reveals sovereign rather than biopower. The forced privatization of excrement was a way of expressing state power. Shit became a political object through the process of making it an individual or private responsibility, making its producers legal proprietors. Property and propriety become linked through the politics of shit.

Poovey's focus is the formation of distinctly modern domains of thought and action in mid-nineteenth-century England. She deploys a method described as "historical epistemology" that allows her to analyze transformations in epistemological fields.[15] Her aim is to see how certain knowledges and protocols became institutionalized, codifying new sets of norms, practices, and boundaries with widespread material effects. As in the *History of Shit* Foucault is present in this text, for transformations in ways of knowing are all about the order of discourse. However, Poovey's state is not the center or singular cause of these transformations, as Laporte argues, but one element in a dense network of technologies, theories, policies, and political disputes that are all implicated in the constitution of new norms and domains of social regulation. Poovey is describing biopower at work.

In her reading of Edwin Chadwick's 1842 *Report on the Sanitary Condition of the Labouring Population of Great Britain*, Poovey shows how, in making sanitation a political issue, domestic norms and personal habits were targeted. In other words, Chadwick's version of "public health" and sanitary reform begins in the working-class home. What Poovey shows in her close reading of this report is that the justification for establishing sanitary conditions in the homes of the poor was primarily moral, despite all the concern about disease and public health. In building a case for the need for sanitation the report problematizes the living habits of the poor. Not only were their household practices suspect due to overcrowding, filth, and debauchery, but also the realm of public space in poor areas was suspect, particularly the street. This was a zone of unimaginable pandemonium where all kinds of boundaries and taboos were violated.[16] This was where dangerous, morally suspect populations lurked: bone pickers, vagrants, and the itinerant poor—groups without homes and often living in and *off* waste.

Chadwick's vision for reform involved a centralized authority, staffed by bureaucratic experts and based on networks of sewerage and drainage systems that would regulate waste along the principles of economic circulation and exchange. His objective, according to Poovey, was a reformed working-class domesticity based on middle-class habits—these were the normative standard that all should aspire to. And the sewer would provide the conditions necessary for such changes in personal behavior and family life. By translating the problem of the working class into the condition of the environment Chadwick justified centralized and preventative measures for the management of shit. But these depended on a logic of individualization and domestication that located the primary identity of the working-class man firmly within the family rather than in class-based associations. Working-class women's capacity to manage the home, and men, was limited by their appalling living conditions; reforming these was where public health coincided with a form of disciplinary individualism in the realm of personal habits.

Osborne is similarly concerned with nineteenth-century public health and its political rationality. Like Poovey he uses Chadwick's sewer vision to develop an argument about normalization. But his analysis focuses on how accounts of the technological achievement of the sewer linked body, city, and governance together. Sewers, drains, privies, and the water supply were conceptualized as "organic," in that they coupled themselves directly and literally to the vital economy of the body.[17] Sanitary engineering allowed for the removal of waste in the name of a purified city, a city purged of all the nuisances that restricted its vital order. It also facilitated a form of indirect government, for drains and flowing water into homes impacted on conduct without any sense of coercion or direct control. Their normalizing impact was not negative or despotic but productive. By linking the standardization of the environment to the vital capacities of the body government established a normative relation. This relation involved the constitution of a distinctively Victorian "vital conscience": the "realisation that the establishment of biological normativity—the ability of the living being to levy norms on the environment—should be one of the aims of political rule."[18] A discourse of naturalization underpinned this. Sanitation had to follow the natural laws of the vital domain, it also naturalized the domestic as a space free from government. The essentially liberal character of this management of shit could be sustained only if natural processes were left to themselves. In this way, sanitation culturally organized the limits and meanings of the "natural." The function of regulation and infrastructure was the government of all those nuisances that posed threats to the security and maintenance of the vital sphere: that field beyond the merely medical that impacted on the wider well-being of the population.

Despite differences in analytic technique and theories of rule, these histories of shit resonate with one another. They allude to the vast and heterogeneous mass of discourses, institutions, social practices, and political processes that have targeted shit from the early modern period on. Human waste may be a universal, but its meanings, its management, and its semiotic and material relations to the body change. It is impossible to think about this sort of waste separate from the forms of knowledge and power that map it into and out of the body; that make defecation a technique of the self. The modern problematization of shit activated a range of different state strategies from edicts to expert inquiries. What links these is the desire to eliminate olfactory and visual contact with this form of waste in order to establish "purity" and "cleanliness" as normative imperatives.

There were, however, significant differences in the sites where waste reform was targeted. Laporte's account shows that in sixteenth-century France the street was the initial space identified as in need of purification. The state forced households to accept responsibility for their waste by outlawing the public disposal of shit on streets. "Public" here was primarily equated with all space beyond the house. This doesn't mean that bodily waste disappeared from streets overnight or that animal manure and other wastes didn't remain an ongoing problem for centuries—it's never been that easy to stop people from using the street as a waste-processing arena. Rather, it means that one of the state's founding conditions was to apply the categories "public" and "private" to shit.

The demand for privies and cesspools within houses inaugurated the individuation and privatization of waste, but it was not until the nineteenth century that waste reformers began to worry about *how* households actually lived with shit. Concern for waste as a public problem was still everywhere evident. Industrial pollution, bad drainage, street garbage, and contaminated water were serious issues in relation to the state of industrializing urban environments, and they were the impetus for major regulatory reforms and infrastructure development. This frenzy of public intervention is significant not simply because of its environmental effects but because of its implications for intimacy. Chadwick's focus on domestic life and his concern to make sure that sanitation had moral—not just hygienic—effects reveals that privacy and its normative dimensions had now become central to the political rationality of biological waste management. It was presumed that leaving families alone with running water and drains made possible all sorts of "good" practices.

What these three histories of shit reveal are the complex transactions between public and private that waste initiated. And while they are useful for understanding how the constitution of modern forms of social administration came to terms with excrement they don't tell us much about how these transactions acquired a visceral intensity. There is a silence about the literal body in both Poovey and Osborne that reduces it to an effect of discourse. Abstracted social bodies or the collective body are their focus, but this makes their accounts of domestic space strangely depopulated. Only Laporte is concerned with how differentiating public and private shit generated new relations to body and self and new affects.

Shifting relations to shit, now that it was kept much closer to home, impacted on subjectivity. Privatization meant domestication, it meant changes to urban architecture and to senses of intimacy and individuality. It meant a new regime of smell in the space of the home. Laporte argues that these practical transformations in relations with shit were fundamental to the organization of the modern subject.[19] While excremental matters were clearly subject to a public-private split in ancient Rome (quite apart from the legendary *cloaca maxima*), Laporte argues that the rituals surrounding excreting in this period did not have the same impact on subjectivity because of the different role of knowledge and power. When the monarchic French state declared *to each his shit* it linked the construction of the privy to a range of other discourses on privacy, particularly the economic. The private realm was demarcated as the site of material *and* waste accumulation. This is when "doing your business" began to acquire symbolic resonances, when both shit and money became inextricably connected to the individual.[20]

Making households retain their shit on-site, making producers masters of their own waste, led to significant transformations in definitions of the intolerable and the economy of the senses. Keeping waste within the space of the family meant that "the apprenticeship of the sense of smell directed all its efforts against the stercus."[21] Laporte shows how shit became the negative referent for the individualized and purified body, and he implicates the state in the same logic, arguing that what the bourgeois subject and the state shared was an inextricable connection to the fate of waste. Their prestige and value depended on establishing *distance* from the basest of human products.

Literal and metaphoric separation from the base is one of the defining markers of modernity's classificatory regimes. But exactly how have our relations with shit and self been transformed by the modern technologies and infrastructure that remove biological waste fast and efficiently? What have sanitation and flushing toilets done to everyday habits, senses of intimacy, and measures of disgust? How has the gradual establishment of the bathroom as a norm of Western domestic architecture impacted on bodies and sensibility? Surely the realization of the contemporary self as a privatized purified body starts in the bathroom, where we confront our particularity as a waste-making organism?

GOING TO THE BATHROOM

In taking a detour to the bathroom the aim here is not architectural or social history but a closer investigation of how this private space of elimination orders our relations to both self and public spheres. If privacy is publicly constituted, as the histories surveyed above show, what is the significance of bathrooms? How is this private space for waste management implicated in the distinction between public and private shit? What sort of micropractices does the bathroom foster, and how do these shape orientations to our bodily waste? Obviously a whole "other" public culture makes the bathroom possible, a culture of engineering and plumbing, massive infrastructural plants and sewerage treatment works. While we are literally connected to this via drains, the state never seems present when we shut the door. This is a result of techniques of invisibility, a technological and aesthetic commitment to disappearance.

These techniques of separation and invisibility have ethical and political effects. The public culture that underpins the bathroom enables the making of a private self. Infrastructure is fundamental to the development of certain conducts and ethical techniques of the self, to the formation of distinctions between clean and dirty, pleasurable and shameful. Rituals of waste management and self-care are now deeply dependent on our attachment to the concrete space of the bathroom, that private realm within the domestic where we are intimate with ourselves.

The normalization of the bathroom as a distinct space for eliminating waste has had dramatic impacts on demarcating the most disgusting and the most private. Plumbing has altered the disciplines of bodies, the ways we manage and map them, and how we experience them as clean. It has been at the heart of shifting discourses of cleanliness and definitions of personal purity. It has also been fundamental to distancing us from any direct role in managing our own waste. While the rich may have always been able to outsource management of their shit, the poor had to deal with their own portable containers. Mass plumbing made distance and separation from your own waste widely accessible. While this is hailed as a triumph of public health and disease management, which it certainly is, the impacts of public waste infrastructure on senses of intimacy and ethical identity are equally significant. Streamlined technologies of elimination make encounters with shit even more charged. If disgust is predicated on "proximity, sight and the closeness of smell and touch, the overwhelming horror that the disgusting object will engulf us," as Elspeth Probyn argues, then much is invested in the efficiency of infrastructure to protect us from the disgusting.[22] The technocratic demand for these services to remove our waste is infused with another, far more visceral, demand: protect the user from any contact, from a proximity to their own waste, that might disturb them. When systems fail and shit gushes up from down below our first response is not to blame the drain or curse the state authority but to protect ourselves from the overwhelming effect, from the horror of contamination.

The logic of bathroom design since the early twentieth century has been "streamlining," an ideology borrowed from manufacturing and privileging efficient and accelerated movement of products through the production cycle.[23] Lupton and Millers' account of streamlining locates it in an emerging modernist concern with waste and the twin obsessions of bodily consumption and economic consumption: "Streamlining performed a surreal conflation of the organic and the mechanical: its seamless skins are fluidly curved yet rigidly impervious to dirt and moisture. The molded forms of streamlining yielded an excretory aesthetic, a material celebration of natural and cultural digestive cycles."[24] In linking the growth of the privatized domestic sphere to the growth of consumption Lupton and Miller show how industry provided a range of powerful metaphors for the organization of the home. The kitchen was a miniature factory, and the bathroom the place where the body's biological production was maintained. Human digestion, based on the consumption of food and the expulsion of waste, was an intimate economy in need of technologies to facilitate efficient processes of elimination.

Since the normalization of the bathroom its specific technologies have continually sought to integrate economic, aesthetic, and hygienic goals. They have has also linked the body to a range of new fixtures and norms of purification. What is significant about these norms is that the standards for personal hygiene, while they may have emerged out of scientifically based public health reforms, have come to far exceed the demands of utility and the functional need for clean bodies. The parallels with housework are strong. As many feminist accounts of the history of labor-saving devices show, domestic technology actually increased the amount of work women did in the home because it was accompanied by rapidly increasing standards of cleanliness.[25]

So too with the bathroom, which is deeply implicated in raising measures of personal cleanliness. Cleaning the self may be easier, but it's done more often and with more anxiety. The motives for this go way beyond the utility of dodging germs; they are caught up in the formation of sensibility, the complex interconnections between sensuousness, ethical telos, and pleasure. If sensibility is a cultivated form of sensuousness, an aesthetic of the self, it is also about the norms and classifications that make these practices meaningful. Making ourselves clean is ethical work; we are transforming the body in relation to a wider moral ethos. We are making a private self that is enmeshed with all the normative measures of privacy and purity swarming around the bathroom. In other words, most of us are far cleaner than we need to be, and most of us have an irrational fear of diseases and contamination. Our rituals of self-purification are linked more to ethical and visceral anxiety than to real biological danger.

Disgust with our own waste, fear of encountering it, cannot be sourced simply to the rise of the bathroom. The modern hygienic imagination and economy of the senses has complex and diverse origins, as we saw in the previous section. But there is no question that the private bathroom has helped organize those fears. Two issues emerge from this: first, the central role of the bathroom in giving the public-private distinction a visceral register. As I've argued, bathrooms established a marked distance from our own waste and inscribed on bodies new classificatory regimes. When these classifications and distinctions are threatened the disgust we experience may seem deeply primal, but it is also social, inextricably caught up in the technological achievement of the bathroom. As a private space this room organizes our most intimate encounters with our own bodies and in the same moment intensifies the force of the affective energies attached to bodily waste.

Second, public infrastructure is implicated in exaggerated senses of personal purity. Bathroom technologies and techniques minimize encounters with shit. They facilitate the myth of absolute separation from waste, on which mastery of the clean self and its borders now increasingly depends. These technologies provide us with gallons of water, an increasingly scarce public resource, to maintain sensibilities and habits that are fundamental to the organization of our prepublic intimate self. While we may pay for access to this resource, and while we may be positioned as consumers in relation to public utilities, we still demand the right to consume as much as we desire because this service is seen as fundamental to our most "natural" self, the clean body.

The paradox is that the very technologies for eradicating shit also, at the same time, affirm and objectify it. Consider the example of a television advertisement for a toilet cleaner. A group of housewives cluster around a toilet listening to a white-coated expert extol the virtues of a new toilet cleaner that requires no additional brushing or scrubbing. "You mean we don't have to touch it?" the women say in unison over and over. The expert repeats his mantra, they repeat their incredulous response. This ad doesn't just capture horror with the toilet; it also captures the visceral registers of disgust. The possibility of contaminating touch demands a streamlined system of waste management and cleaning practices that make no physical or ethical demands on the waste-making body. Without this chemical protection the boundaries of the private self are dangerously vulnerable.

While this ad, like many others in the same genre, upholds the fantasy that the purified private self must be protected from its waste, other examples represent the bathroom as a space of luxury consumption and desire centered around an endless availability of pure water. In 2003 Sydney introduced water restrictions, and several local governments implemented regulations demanding mandatory dual-flush toilets in all new developments. The outcry from certain outraged constituents was furious. How could the state control how much water consumers could use to eliminate their waste? Surely this was an infringement of basic consumer rights, especially when these water-saving toilets were occasionally inefficient, producing confrontations that consumers didn't want to have? Using gallons and gallons of clean water to eliminate their waste protected them from this possibility. Why should they be denied access to water when, as they claimed: "We're paying for it!"

Here is the private subject in the bathroom accusing the state of restricting his or her freedom as a consumer and putting his or her most intimate sense of self at risk. The rhetoric of ecological responsibility, of scarce public resources and the need for restraint, is refused. For this is the rhetoric of citizenship and civic values, of collective identification with the notion of public good and the environment. To be a consumer is to be able to realize individual and private desires not just in the mall but also in the bathroom. It is to see the purchase of goods and services as integral to the making and maintenance of personal identity. Whether these goods and services come from the state or multinational corporations is not as crucial as the fact that they are purchased. Buying things makes us members of a market, makes us expect choice, makes us demand our right to have our needs satisfied. If certain practices of waste management are fundamental to senses of purity and identity then individuals must be free to consume all that it takes to sustain these. In this example the heavily subsidized state provision of public waste infrastructure rubs up against restrictions on domestic water use and the demand that consumers restrain themselves in the interest of the environment. Water users are a public and consumers at the same time, and the tensions between these two subjectivities underpin these protests.

Advertisements for toilet cleaners and protests about dual-flushing toilets are two moments in which we can see the complex interconnections between self, state, and market. While the normalization of the bathroom has been fundamental to modern experiences of privacy and a prepublic purified self, it has also distanced us from waste in the name of public health and infrastructural efficiency. While these technocratic achievements cannot be underestimated, they also need to be understood in terms of their impacts on

subjectivity and the experience of the public-private distinction. Despite sanitation's massively networked connections from public waste facilities to private homes it is not experienced as state intervention. It is just the hidden
linchpin of our most intimate rituals of self-care. Water flows in, shit flows
out, where from and where to we hardly care. The thing is that the flows are
maintained, that our bathroom *works* to protect us from encountering our
waste, so that certain ethical and aesthetic sensibilities that are fundamental to
the making of the purified private self will be not be threatened.

POO PROTESTS

How then is the bathroom and the streamlined elimination of shit implicated
in a wider politics of waste? As I've argued, bathrooms help produce our most
intimate sense of self, but this intimacy depends on a diverse network of technologies and public resources. When access to these is restricted and consumers protest, the political object at stake is privacy and a purified self. In
moving now to two very different examples of political activism around human waste I aim to examine what is at stake in protests whose focus is shit in
public. How do these protests configure the place of waste in the public-private
distinction? Does the formation of activist publics around shit necessarily involve indifference to the particularity of ourselves, as Warner argues? Do intimate waste practices get ignored or mobilized? Two great moments in the
politics of shit open up these questions—Sydney's famous POOO Parades in
the late 1980s and the ongoing toilet festivals of Mumbai.[26]

In January 1989 Sydney's leading newspaper, the *Sydney Morning Herald*,
began running a series of investigative reports on the state of Sydney's
beaches.[27] These highlighted extensive water pollution, evident not only in the
filth washed up onshore but also in reports of sick fish and sick swimmers.
The primary target was the Water Board, the government agency involved in
managing Sydney's water supply and human waste. Ocean outfalls and their
failings were identified as the source of widespread ocean pollution. And no
wonder; since white settlement all drains built in Sydney have pointed sea-
ward. The first sewers, built in the 1850s, drained raw sewage into the harbor,
and this use of natural water as a waste treatment facility has remained largely
unchanged since. For government waste management organizations the value
of the ocean is not its recreational or real estate possibilities but its seemingly
unlimited potential as a site of elimination.

The 1989 exposé led by the media accused the Water Board of covering up the facts of serious ocean contamination and misleading the public. Surfline, the Water Board's daily report on the state of the beaches, was exposed as based on nothing more than visual observation. Scientific analysis of water samples revealed a very different story—high levels of faecal coliform, viruses, and highly toxic industrial waste. Outraged reaction spread, the Surf Lifesaving Association threatened to remove its volunteers from beach patrol, fish sales plummeted, swimmers deserted the beach, and doctors reported increased levels of illness among people who had recently surfed. Meanwhile, the media kept up the pressure, branding the whole issue "Watergate."

In this context the Water Board struggled to retain public credibility. Since the late 1970s it had been planning to build extended ocean outfalls in order to manage increased pressure on the sewerage system and increased pollution. Vigorous debate had surrounded this proposal, much of it devoted to disputes over the environmental effects of outfalls and the interpretation of scientific studies. Public calls for alternative and more environmentally friendly strategies for dealing with shit were met with claims that they were too expensive. The Water Board argued that ocean outfalls were the cheapest solution for dealing with a city's shit; more environmentally sustainable options would cost residents far more and generate significant resistance. The Water Board mobilized scientific "evidence" to show that extended deepwater outfalls were environmentally fine and that effluent would behave just as predicted and that no other treatment was necessary.

But a group of skeptical environmental and community groups refused to buy this; effluent wasn't that obedient, especially when there was no secondary treatment. The Board's refusal to consider this objection in planning the outfalls meant that the ocean was, once again, regarded as a dumping ground; the Board's bureaucrats argued that currents, dilution, and dispersal were adequate alternatives to comprehensive treatment before discharge. Other lobby groups raised the issue of industrial waste, the illegal and toxic substances coursing through drains: What would extended outfalls do about this? Stop the Ocean Pollution (STOP) and People Opposed to Ocean Outfalls (POOO), two small activist groups, campaigned as effectively as they could during the 1980s struggling to get their position in the media, but the Water Board had a massive public relations unit and a very cozy relationship with the press—until 1989, that is.

The debate about ocean outfalls and contaminated waters took off when the press finally challenged the Water Board about its technocratic ethos and lack of accountability. But this challenge escalated into a mass campaign only because the activist groups already established, STOP and POOO, grabbed the opportunity to mobilize public anger about state lies and state pollution. In late 1988 POOO organized a little-publicized rally at Manly beach that attracted five thousand people on a rainy day. In March 1989 another event was planned. Called "Turn Back the Tide," it was envisaged as a rock concert on Bondi beach, with a crowd of 50,000 the optimistic expectation; 240,000 people showed up.

The phenomenal success of the "Turn Back the Tide" concert surprised organizers, government, media, and, most of all, the Water Board. It was no longer possible to claim that the issue was a media attack; a mass rally of nearly a quarter of a million people signaled a real groundswell of support. It signaled a public formed by an ongoing media debate, emerging at an event as a mass assembly, linked not just by visibility and common action but also by a common anxiety.

What kind of public was produced at the "Turn Back the Tide" concert, and how did it work? Only by answering these questions is it possible to reflect on exactly how shit became a political object in this campaign and whether a different future for shit was imagined. Warner's account of the dynamics of publics and counterpublics is invaluable here. He meticulously outlines the discursive and political operations of *a* public as distinct from *the* public. His aim is to understand how publics are historically formed, their crucial place in the modern social landscape, and their role in constructing social worlds. The mass of bodies that gathered on Bondi beach was a public organized, brought into being, by discourse. Press reports, television news, and radio talk shows created a public merely through the fact that people all over Sydney gave the various discourses on ocean pollution some attention. No matter how minimal, listening, reflecting, or glancing at the headlines are all ways of participating in a public and accepting being addressed by its terms.[28]

The "Turn Back the Tide" concert reflects another of Warner's premises: stranger sociability. If a public is a relation among strangers, then the bodies gathered at Bondi performed their public belonging not by sharing a common identity but by accepting and inhabiting the rhetoric of public address. Participants' private concerns about oceans contaminated with shit were experienced as resonating with complete strangers. In this way the discourses circulating were ambiguously personal *and* impersonal. Warner says of public speech that "we might recognize ourselves as addressees but it is equally important that we remember that the speech was addressed to indefinite others."[29] This performative dimension of publics, this sense of their membership being active, free, voluntary, and noninstitutionalized, set the "Turn Back the Tide" event apart from the wider social movement of environmentalism. While pollution was a central point of discursive mobilization, and while various environmental and activist groups were involved in mounting the campaign, the public formed could not be described as sharing a common history or political ideology. Those who turned up at Bondi beach could not be described as a "rent-a-crowd" or the usual suspects of "mad greenies." As a public they didn't preexist, they were called into being by a vision of a contaminated world.

Warner also argues that processes of public formation do not involve persuasion, as this presumes that a public already exists, waiting to be convinced by rational discussion—and that individuals in that public will all have the same reading of available discourses. The problem with the assumption of preexisting publics is that it excludes the poetic or textual qualities of discourse. Sense and reason are privileged rather than the play of meaning, emotion, and the expressive possibilities of public speech.

As one of the founders of POOO said, when interviewed about why he set up the organization: "Dumping shit and everything else in the ocean just seems wrong, I don't want to surf in shit."[30] Not a lot of poetry here but definitely a sense of disgust and moral unease. There is no question that the discourses surrounding "Turn Back the Tide" and the POOO Parades were often driven by an affective horror or mass disgust. This affective register gave expression to a counterdiscourse about shit in public that challenged the Water Board's notions of technocratic efficiency and scientific evidence. And this was the source of their force. The rash of cartoons depicting people diving into toilet bowls, or lifeguards hauling a roll of toilet paper into the surf instead of a rescue rope, were evidence of how an alternative discourse about sewers began circulating. This discourse created a different image of the issue by making explicit the link between bathrooms and the beach. By exposing the literal connection between private waste practices and public space, the "Turn Back the Tide" public produced another set of understandings of the outfall crisis. Their vision of a poisoned world, of the ocean as a waste dump, didn't just speak to a deep anxiety about boundaries collapsing, to a sense of mourning for the archaic value of the ocean, it also gave voice to an array of alternative strategies for managing shit.

As the issue grew the press began publishing different ideas for dealing with Sydney's shit. All kinds of weird and wonderful ecological approaches surfaced. These included giant sewerage farms out west converting shit into agricultural fertilizer, decentralized waste treatment works, and the creation of artificial wetlands in the midst of urban sprawl. All of these alternatives mobilized popular expertise. They involved creative, imaginative solutions driven not simply by the technical problem of managing a large city's shit but also by an ethical imperative to do this sustainably and in ways that did not involve the exploitation of the ocean. The Water Board's domination of the issue, its desire to reduce it to an engineering problem, was contested by a counterdiscourse that circulated widely and that radically expanded the terms of the public debate. This counterdiscourse often included the expression of a range of emotions, from anger to disgust to grief to hilarity; it acknowledged the visceral dangers implicit in all waste management. The credibility given to alternative ecological worldviews (usually dismissed as the work of cranks) and the linking of the most private and intimate waste practice, defecating, to public space and the public sphere—both were part of an emergent counterpublic. And the effect of this counterpublic was to problematize shit and its public management, to establish a different and progressive ethico-political framing of the issue.

But it didn't last long—this fleeting counterpublic was soon coopted by the disciplines of political negotiation, and the terms of its discourse were gradually reduced to a technocratic agenda set by the state. The list of demands POOO put to government and the Water Board after the "Turn Back the Tide" concert included removing all toxic waste from sewers, halting all future ocean outfall construction, and classifying oceans under the Clean Waters Act. There was nothing on the list about initiating some of the alternative strategies for ecologically sustainable management of shit that had been proposed and nothing about changing what went on in bathrooms. The ocean was constituted as in need of protection, the public authority was constituted as in need of reform and accountability, but private waste practices went unchallenged. Despite the scatological vision of beaches and bathrooms being intimately connected (swimming in shit, surfing in toilets); despite the recognition of the toilet and drain as technologies not for managing waste but for dumping it;

despite all these transgressive representations of shit in public that the POOO parades and other events conjured up, intimate waste practices and their excessive use of resources were not regarded as part of a reform strategy. The politics of the possible overruled a vision of other ways of living with waste. Those present at the "Turn Back the Tide" concert were ultimately unable to confront the particularities of themselves. Their privacy was deemed outside the scope of the public campaign.

The Toilet Festivals of Mumbai and other Indian cities are a very different example of the politics of shit. Described by Appadurai as an example of deep democracy, they too involve a spirit of transgression and bawdy modes of public address, but their political aim is quite different.[31] Initiated by the Alliance, a group of activist organizations working on urban poverty in Mumbai, the Toilet Festivals involve the exhibition and inauguration of working public toilets designed by and for the urban poor and often timed to coincide with visits from various state and aid officials.[32] Appadurai's analysis of these festivals begins with an account of the humiliation of shitting in public, an inevitable and shaming reality for millions of Indians living in urban slums without sanitation. Quite apart from the public health risks of shitting without good sewerage systems and running water, this reality involves the most fundamental lack of privacy. As Appadurai argues, the risks of shitting in full public view are not just biological, they're symbolic. The inability to establish distance from their own waste denies slum dwellers the most basic sense of dignity and status. Shit confirms their victimization and poverty.

Contesting this means managing shit in a way that reduces health risks and confers dignity—hence, do-it-yourself sanitation. By designing their own toilets, building them, and using them, slum dwellers link technical innovation to a democratic practice focused on establishing the minimal conditions for privacy and a sense of intimate selfhood. In this change in the technical management of waste, "the condition of poverty moves from abjection to subjectivation."[33] The political object at stake here is not simply public health and basic waste management, it is also privacy. And what gives these festivals such force, according to Appadurai, is the fact that access to privacy also inaugurates a visible citizenship, it makes entry into the public sphere possible.

Can these two cases of the politics of shit illuminate each other, despite massive political and economic differences, despite vast variation in the place of shit in measures of a good life in Mumbai and Bondi? The Toilet Festivals confirm Laporte's insistence that shit is crucial to the making of modern sub-jectivity; that shit is at the heart of public and private distinctions and the formation of a purified, private self. Although it was never acknowledged, the Bondi POOO protesters were defending their privacy. They were defending the necessity of a clear, unambiguous separation from their shit in the name of stable moral frameworks: clean-dirty, self-waste. Swimming in shit undoes this classificatory regime and the security of the self that depends on it. In making ocean outfalls the focus of political action, the POOO protesters were taking private waste rituals as given, as beyond question. The demand for un-contaminated oceans targeted the state as a polluter but not the self. The technology of streamlined elimination that the sewer represents means that the minute bodily waste disappears the self is no longer implicated or re-sponsible for its management—until it returns and becomes impossible to ignore.

Sewers transform shit to effluent, from private waste to public problem. Streamlined removal facilitates literal and moral distance from our bodily waste, and most of the time this distance contributes to an ethical blindness about its management. Although the carnivalesque atmosphere of the POOO parades made much of shit's role in disturbing the private-public distinction, the vision for reform was unable to sustain this disturbance and use it as a force for new practices. Ultimately, public waste management was the prob-lem, *not* rituals of privacy.

In the toilet festivals the demand for minimal public waste infrastructure is fundamentally linked to the right to privacy. Shitting in public, living their lives in perpetual visibility, Appadurai argues, actually renders slum dwellers *invisible* to the state. In claiming the right to privacy, slum dwellers participate in a politics of recognition. To have privacy is to exist in the eyes of the state, and this is the starting point for making claims for basic public services. Pri-vacy is the political object at stake in these campaigns. It is defined as the abil-ity to establish distance from one's shit, to be separate from its contaminating influence. And this minimal privacy is seen as publicly constituted. The ca-pacity to make a private self, to manage one's waste in a way that produces subjectivity rather than shame, to bracket off certain intimate practices from the gaze of others, is a fundamental process of distinction that anyone living with a bathroom takes as given. It inaugurates a public personhood. The rad-ical claim of the toilet festivals, to make waste a private matter, is inseparable from the demand for basic public provision. Or, to put this another way, in the toilet festivals the personal is political.

For the POOO public the personal was not political. The conditions for privacy and separation from shit that the state provided were not challenged. Rather, it was what the state did with shit once it assumed responsibility for it that was under attack. And so the outfalls were built, further offshore and deeper but still pouring thousands of gallons of effluent into the ocean every day. The fleeting counterpublic formed by the horror of shit along shorelines, grease in the breakers, viruses in the sand, dissipated once the Water Board was called into account and agreed to certain modifications to its technocratic vision. Privacy was not called into account. Sydneysiders' inability or refusal to imagine a different way of living with their waste meant the their senses of purity and decorum were never at risk. Public infrastructure would still be there to protect them from themselves.

Bondi and Mumbai are a long way apart and in many senses difficult to compare. But the differences between them are suggestive. When the "Turn Back the Tide" counterpublic imagined a world in which oceans were not exploited as waste treatment facilities, the possibilities of an ecological citizenship were glimpsed. Here was a public disgusted by environmental disintegration, willing to contest state authority and advocate for oceans. The only problem was this vision did not extend to their intimate practices of waste management; any critical reflection on their personal ethics of waste was excluded. The right to privacy, to all the resource-hungry waste habits that sustain a private personhood, was separated from their public performance as concerned and disgusted citizens. In the Mumbai slums privation and powerlessness are the norm, not neoliberal notions of privacy. Human waste is one marker of this. Getting it effectively managed to reduce disease shows how do-it-yourself governmentality inaugurates a self able to be minimally recognized by the state. By refusing to shit in public, members of the Mumbai Alliance use waste to create a private personhood and with it a nascent citizenship: different habits, different ways in which waste is implicated in the distinctions between a public and private self.

NOTES

A version of this essay was published as "Shit in Public" in *Australian Humanities Review*, April 2004, at www.lib.latrobe.edu.au/AHR/archive/Issue-April-2004/hawkins.html.

1. Michael Warner, *Publics and Counterpublics* (New York: Zone Books, 2002), 160.

2. Warner, *Publics and Counterpublics*, see especially chapter 1.

3. I have explored these ideas in more depth in my essay "Down the Drain: Shit and the Politics of Disturbance," in *Culture and Waste: The Creation and Destruction of Value*, ed. Gay Hawkins and Stephen Muecke (Lanham, MD: Rowman and Littlefield, 2002).

4. William Connolly, *Why I Am Not a Secularist* (Minneapolis: University of Minnesota Press, 1999), xviii.

5. The best example of this would be Martin Melosi's *Garbage in Cities: Refuse, Reform and the Environment, 1880–1980* (Texas: A & M University Press, 1981).

6. Michel Foucault, *The History of Sexuality*, vol. 1, trans. R. Hurley (New York: Penguin Books, 1981).

7. Catherine Mills, "Biopower, Liberal Eugenics and Nihilism" (unpublished paper presented at BIOS—A Politics and Technology Research Workshop, University of New South Wales, August 6, 2004).

8. Dominique Laporte, *History of Shit*, trans. N. Benabid and R. El-Khoury (Cambridge, MA: MIT Press, 2000).

9. Mary Poovey, *Making a Social Body* (Chicago: University of Chicago Press, 1995); Thomas Osborne, "Security and Vitality: Drains, Liberalism and Power in the Nineteenth Century," in *Foucault and Political Reason*, ed. A. Barry, T. Osborne, N. Rose (Chicago: University of Chicago Press, 1996).

10. Warner, *Publics and Counterpublics*, 62.

11. My argument here draws on an earlier paper cited in note 3: Hawkins, *Down the Drain*.

12. Laporte, *History of Shit*, 112.

13. Laporte, *History of Shit*, 40.

14. Laporte, *History of Shit*, 46.

15. Poovey, *Making a Social Body*, 5.

16. Poovey, *Making a Social Body*, 123.

17. Osborne, "Security and Vitality," 114.

18. Osborne, "Security and Vitality," 116.

19. The gradual disqualification of smell and the ascendance of sight in the hierarchy of the senses are well known. It is the driving narrative in Alain Corbin's account of the decline of the olfactory sense in *The Foul and the Fragrant*, in Freud's arguments about the upright position and the civilizing impulse, and in Norbert Elias's account of how manners and sensibilities shift from the promiscuous to the modest in *The Civilizing Process*. What Laporte adds to these accounts is an insistence that shit is at the heart of the constitution of a modern "I."

20. Laporte, *History of Shit*, 45–47.

21. Laporte, *History of Shit*, 65.

22. Elspeth Probyn, *Carnal Appetites* (London: Routledge, 2000), 131.

23. Ellen Lupton and J. Abbott Miller, *The Bathroom, the Kitchen and the Aesthetics of Waste* (Cambridge, MA: MIT Visual Arts Center, 1992).

24. Lupton and Miller, *Aesthetics of Waste*, 2.

25. See, for example, Suellen Hoy, *Chasing Dirt* (Oxford: Oxford University Press, 1995).

26. Arjun Appadurai, "Deep Democracy," *Public Culture* 14, no. 1 (Winter 2002).

27. My analysis here draws heavily on Sharon Beder's excellent account of these events in *Toxic Fish and Sewer Surfing* (Sydney: Allen and Unwin, 1989).

28. Warner, *Publics and Counterpublics*, 87.

29. Warner, *Publics and Counterpublics*, 77.

30. Sheila Browne, "Why POOO Raises a Stink," *Sydney Morning Herald*, February 15, 1990.

31. Appadurai, "Deep Democracy," 39.

32. Appadurai, "Deep Democracy," 39.

33. Appadurai, "Deep Democracy," 39.

4

A Dumped Car

I think of how little we can hold in mind, how everything is constantly lapsing into oblivion with every extinguished life, how the world is, as it were, draining itself, in that the history of countless places and objects which themselves have no power of memory is never heard, never described or passed on.

—*W. G. Sebald, Austerlitz*

In writing about loss W. G. Sebald reminds us of the importance of detritus. For him, abandoned places and things have the power to reveal the reality of vanished lives. But this power is rarely acknowledged; instead, the world seems to be "draining itself." Why is this metaphor of the drain so unsettling? Could it be because drains facilitate such efficient disappearance? It's easy to forget things when elimination is so streamlined, when there is no possibility of careful deliberation. But do all the things we discard lapse into oblivion, drained of power and memory? Or do they outlive us, accumulating across the landscape, dumped but certainly not disappeared?

Don DeLillo finds the answers to these questions in the open landfill. The landfill is a monumental world of soaring garbage, mountains and valleys, trucks and roads with its own distinct smell and soundscape; a place that organizes and frames things *as* waste. A place where "all the appetites and hankerings, the sodden second thoughts came runneling out, the things you ardently wanted and then did not."[1] The open landfill is a landscape in its own right, a "dump" where we confront the forceful presence of things just sinking into themselves, broken and decaying, no longer bound by taxonomy or value.

DeLillo's world isn't drained of things; it's drowning in them, groaning under the weight of excess and obsolescence. In *Underworld* waste generates various new circuits of value: spectacular landscapes, art made out of redundant B52s, and the gangster capitalism of the garbage industry.[2] It also fuels an almost hallucinatory version of Cold War America, in which—despite his fascination with rubbish and waste management—DeLillo seems somehow blind to the materiality of waste. By overstating the case with too much awe and spectacle DeLillo does not so much remember waste as redeem it. His depiction of a Staten Island landfill creates a world in which the monstrous and majestic inhumanness of waste dwarfs the human. The landfill is a landscape visible from outer space, it is a testament to the persistence of waste and to its overwhelming presence in the era of the mass commodity form. DeLillo echoes a familiar trope in much environmentalism about the burdens of materialism. The underworld of capitalist accumulation is waste, the underhistory of American society is waste. By representing waste as things that cannot be removed, that will always return, DeLillo *others* waste, using it as the mirror of the American soul.

Sebald, in contrast, sticks closely to the qualitative character of abandoned things. Consider his reverie on a pile of mattresses:

> Histories, for instance, like those of the straw mattresses which lay, shadow-like, on the stacked plank beds and which had become thinner and shorter because the chaff in them disintegrated over the years, shrunken—and now, in writing this, I do remember that such an idea occurred to me at the time—as if they were the mortal frames of those who once lay there in that darkness.[3]

Sebald doesn't situate these abandoned objects in an epic historical narrative. He doesn't fetishize them; rather, he performs a kind of memory work. He apprehends the mattresses in their mundanity, and in the process they become the bodies that lay on them. Sebald gives the mattresses the power of memory.

These are two very different reflections on the nature of wasted objects; Sebald's profoundly melancholic and DeLillo's paranoid and apocalyptic.[4] Their differences are instructive. While DeLillo documents the presence of waste everywhere in overconsuming cultures, Sebald draws attention to the materiality of abandoned objects, reminding us of how little we notice them. For my purposes Sebald is more suggestive. Unlike DeLillo he is not interested in waste as a majestic landscape emblematic of capitalist social relations. Sebald rejects the "landscape function" for waste and all that it entails: the inevitable pull of aesthetics, the constitution of the environment as passively awaiting a human gaze, and human desecration. Instead, he contemplates waste as *things*. He acknowledges the materiality of waste and its ontological instability.

In exploring the dynamic exchanges between subjects and objects, Sebald captures the translations and displacements that shape human relations with the material world. Ornaments, utensils, dumped car wrecks, mattresses—objects that have outlived their former owners—have what Bill Brown calls "history *in* them."[5] Their dislocation and uncanny presence as remainders makes the traces of their former uses and human attachments visible. Sebald's abandoned things speak of the full magnitude of what happened. He uses cultural debris to confront the past not as moral lesson but as a source of philosophical reflection about loss, destruction, and grief. His "method," if you can call it that, is a powerful evocation of Walter Benjamin's materialist history. For Sebald, like Benjamin, is interested in the phenomenological hermeneutics of cultural debris.[6] Sebald shows what can happen when you notice waste, when you pay close attention to its presence. Suddenly, discarded objects appear animate and able to make claims on us. By refusing to other waste, to reduce it to structure or metaphor, Sebald implicates waste's materiality in questions of affect and ethics.

Could the recognition of waste as *things* change our relations with it? Could it lead to different forms of materialism less concerned with the vagaries of desire or disposability? What would an ethics of waste mean for our material habitus, for how we actually live with things? This chapter explores these questions. While its inspiration is Sebald, its examples are two extraordinary films: Agnes Varda's *The Gleaners and I* and Walpiri Media's *Bush Mechanics*. In both these films people engage with waste. While their motivation is often scarcity and need, the material practices they invent involve an openness to the thingness of waste. It is the possibility of transformation and misuse that makes waste available to other systems of objectification. But you have to be willing to see and feel this. Inventing a new materialism involves a responsiveness to objects that is mutually transformative of both people and things.[7] Waste captures the attention not simply of those in desperate need but also of those able to imagine different uses, able to reanimate it. This is where necessity meets creativity and where ethics meet imagination.

Before we look at these films, the value of thinking about waste as things needs to be considered more carefully. This takes us into the realm of material culture and thing theory. Theories of material culture show how history and biography apply to things. They show how the work of consumption and exchange creates value and how material forms can be coded and recoded to satisfy human needs and desires. This work is invaluable for reminding us how human uses give objects instrumental status. But is there a realm of thingness that exists beyond this material object world? Is there a point where things cannot be reduced to objects, where their presence is asserted in ways that disrupt their object status? And could this nascent thingness be a potential source of different, more ecologically aware practices?

According to Bill Brown, we glimpse thingness in irregularities of exchange, in moments when objects stop working for us, or when we are not quite sure how to identify: all situations that could easily describe waste.[8] These experiences involve an encounter with the anterior physicality of the world, with the sensuous presence that exceeds the materialization and utilization of objects. These are experiences of objects asserting themselves as things, when things provoke and incite, when they capture our attention and demand to be noticed. And in these chance interruptions, these "occasions of contingency," as Brown calls them, different relations surface: "The story of objects asserting themselves as things, then, is the story of a changed relation to the human subject and thus the story of how the thing really names less an object than a particular subject-object relation."[9]

This approach shifts the focus from material culture's anthropological inflections to phenomenology and philosophy. Brown is concerned less with the social life of objects than with how things become "recognizable, representable and exchangeable to begin with," with the mutual constitution of human subject and inanimate object.[10] Elizabeth Grosz's account of the thing takes a similar approach. Like Brown, she is interested in how things assert themselves and how we become enmeshed with them, and she draws on pragmatist philosophers to make her case. Darwin, William James, Bergson, Rorty, and Deleuze all, in different ways, put questions of action and practice at the center of ontology. Here the thing features as a resource for being. We make things with it, leave our trace on it, but this does not mean that the thing is subordinate to human action. For the thing has a "life" of its own that we must accommodate in our activities. "The thing poses questions to us, questions about our needs and desires, questions above all of action: the thing is our provocation to action and is itself a result of our action."[11] Although Grosz doesn't argue this, in her schema things are irrevocably implicated in ethics. For if things pose questions to us then they must also be capable of making us consider what we do.

What, then, of waste? Theories of material culture show us the role of circulation and use in the creation and destruction of value; they illuminate the human and social contexts of objects in motion. But what happens when objects stop moving, when they get stuck on the verge abandoned or when they turn into urban debris? Thing theory explores how the latency of thingness might surface in these moments when objectification breaks down. For if the thing is always a kind of remainder, so too is waste, hence the potential of waste to remind us of the liminality between useful and useless, object and thing. If we noticed waste as things, what sort of new material relations and practices might this trigger? When waste is framed as dead objects and relegated to its proper place in the dump or garbage truck it often fails to provoke. It poses no questions to us because it has been regulated and rendered passive and out of sight. Waste as dead objects throws up few possibilities, but waste as things is full of promise, full of the possibilities of becoming a resource for being.

GETTING TO WASTE

Objects die. And while I'm interested in their afterlife, the causes of death matter. When people classify something as waste they are deciding that they no longer want to be connected to it. Sometimes this is a big decision and sometimes it's not. The plastic cup chucked in the bin walking out of the football stadium is a relief to be rid of. The short life of the disposable object is over—easy come, easy go. The favorite chair handed down from grandparents and now unstable and beyond repair is hard to throw out. It's useless but still connected to the self via circuits of memory and affect. The conversion of objects into waste is complex and complicated. There is a multiplicity of pathways to the limit point at which all function and value are exhausted.

While all cultures need distinctions between valued and valueless, there are multiple and diverse subclassifications within both these categories. Some objects are valueless but we still hang on to them. They are no longer used but their lingering presence in the garage doesn't threaten us. These things aren't unsettling because they are out of sight, occupying a residual status in the microclassifications of rubbish. Then there are the valueless things that we encounter all the time: the dumpster behind the supermarket full of boxes of overripe pears, the perfectly functional but tattered sofa on the pavement; things classified as waste because they are wrecked, in excess of demand, or no longer desired, but still visible in our everyday movements through urban space. Other things are negatively valued; they threaten the stability of self, and we do all we can to eliminate them and render them invisible. As the previous chapter argues, negatively valued waste like shit challenges boundaries and symbolic order, hence its potential to be extremely disturbing. In this chapter it's the valueless rather than the negatively valued, the discarded but still visible waste and rubbish, that is the focus.

Recent writing on material culture has begun to focus on the conversion processes from valued to valueless. While transformations in uses, significations, and values have always been a central concern in this field, the transformations involved in the production of waste and rubbish have been somewhat overlooked. Gavin Lucas, like Nicky Gregson and Louise Crewe, notes the relative lack of interest in waste within studies of material culture.[12] While theorists have been happy to see waste as a historically changing category or as a source of archaeological insight, they have been less interested in comprehending it as a distinct classification or form of value.[13] Now, there is an interesting body of work beginning to investigate how objects become rubbish, how they get to the end of value. My reading of this work identifies several key themes that are worth setting down. The aim is to understand what frames of meaning shape our relations with rubbish and how open these are to transformation. Any possibility of a new materialism and ethics of waste must begin with a different recognition of discarded material. While environmentalism recognizes this in the demand that everybody "reduce, reuse, and recycle," this is only the beginning of the story. The imperative to manage our waste better or avoid the "waste stream" altogether doesn't really get to the heart of how we might come to live differently with things.

The first theme that emerges in recent work in material culture on waste is how reluctant many people are to transfer objects into this category. The rise of a biographical approach to things has documented the myriad of taxonomies, uses, and valuing regimes that objects can move through before they reach the end of their lives, if they ever do. Kopytoff describes the process in this way:

> In the homogenised world of commodities, an eventful biography of a thing becomes the story of the various singularisations of it, of classification and reclassification in an uncertain world of categories whose importance shifts with every minor change of context. As with persons, the drama here lies in the uncertainties of valuation and identity.[14]

The creativity of material practices, the constant reincorporation of objects into new classes and systems of exchange and use, makes any essentialist claims about the identity and fixed life cycle of things difficult to sustain. Accounts of the history of things, of their social lives, show that games of value are hard to finish, many things just want to keep on playing. This means that waste, as a point of absolute separation and dematerialization, is often a radical conversion process.

Two studies stand out. Gregson and Crewe's detailed cultural geography of secondhand cultures documents the rich array of classificatory systems and practices that steer things away from the finality of waste. Junk, secondhand, collectables, and retro are a few of the many classifications used to manage and recirculate goods after first-stage consumption.[15] Each classification reflects a specific set of economic, moral, aesthetic, and valuing regimes that work to move objects into various spaces, from the garage to the junk shop to the charity bin; and into different modes of exchange, from philanthropy to barter.

Lucas's study of disposability and dispossession looks at archaeological analyses of waste and comes to similar conclusions: reuse and revaluation are extensive, particularly in relation to things such as clothing, domestic appliances, and furnishings. Dispossession, or the active decision to remove something from one's life and discard it, is as complex a process as possession.[16] What both these studies show is that getting to waste is complicated, and the importance of a material culture perspective is the way it has begun to document this. Gregson and Crewe's research reveals an extraordinary liminal zone in which objects are suspended in time-space awaiting revaluation, their biographies stretched potentially to infinity.[17]

But a biographical perspective cannot evade the question of *de*valuation. Things still get chucked out, constantly, without thought. The ritual of putting out the garbage is one of the markers of the temporality of everyday life. It is also one of the key ways in which we acknowledge the zero degree of value. We need rubbish, as Michael Thompson argues, not just because purification rituals are important to boundaries but also because systems of value depend on a limit point.[18] Thompson's work in *Rubbish Theory* is important because he shows how rubbish makes possible transformations in use and value. Without a category of rubbish it is impossible to generate new and unexpected structures of value. It is impossible for value to move or change. Thompson identifies two major categories of value to which objects are assigned: "transient" for those things that are decreasing in value over time and "durable" for objects whose value increases over time.[19] Most consumer goods would be in the transient category, antiques or art in the durable. The location of different objects in these categories shapes human relationships and uses. The kids can romp around on the worn-out sofa because it's on the downhill slide of value, they can't touch the deco vase on the mantelpiece because it's precious and irreplaceable.

Value is a product of social processes, not the intrinsic properties of things. Just because things decay and wear out does not mean that they automatically lose value. Signs of aging and use can contribute to increased or auratic value. In the same sense the shiny new plastic cup appears to us as imminent rubbish; disposability makes transient value strikingly visible. The fact of malleability and transformation in value is evidence that objects are not locked into categories because of their material qualities. It is *how* their materiality is apprehended and used that is the key to value and its transformation. The question is: What is the role of rubbish in this process of shifting value?

Thompson argues that rubbish is central to accounts of the social control of value because it provides the path for the seemingly impossible transfer of objects from transience to durability. Rubbish is a covert category in between the transient and the durable that functions as a valueless limbo in which, at some point, the object may be rediscovered, given new value, and transferred into the category of durability. The examples Thompson uses to develop this argument are decayed inner-city housing that is gentrified and an obscure kitsch Victorian artifact, the Stevengraph, which suddenly became a collector's item in the mid-1960s. In the case of the Stevengraph two key factors were involved in the transformation of value. First, as economic value increased so too did aesthetic value in the form of research, scholarly publications, exhibitions, and museum acquisitions. And second, men controlled the transfer of value from rubbish to durable. While the Victorian purchase and display of Stevengraphs was a feminine occupation, men dominated the transfer from rubbish to collectable. They wrote the authoritative books, organized the exhibitions, and ran the sales. Changes in value are caught up in wider patterns of distinction and status.[20]

The significance of Thompson's theory is that it offers an explanation of the structural role of rubbish in formations of value. Worthlessness is the condition of possibility for objects to move between different categories. And this movement or process of malleability is grounded *not* in the intrinsic properties of things but in the new and unexpected uses and functions that people bring to them. However, while Thompson acknowledges that innovation and creativity are crucial to the flexibility of value, he doesn't pursue this. John Frow does in a brief but incisive reading of *Rubbish Theory*.[21] Frow develops Thompson's argument by showing how transformations of value are fundamental to person-thing relations: "Objects don't simply occupy a realm of objecthood over and against the human: they translate human interests, carry and transform desire and strategies."[22] For Frow, function is a product of use, and the potential uses of things (appropriate and inappropriate) are infinitely variable; "No single game exhausts their function."[23]

Frow's nuanced account of person-thing relations is concerned with conversion processes, how things pass from one state to another. While this is the central issue in many studies of material culture, Frow's interest is not in tracking the career of objects, their circulation through different uses and patterns of exchange. Rather, he is concerned with understanding the specific *kinds of recognition* that mediate distinctions between person and thing.[24] His analysis of several different examples shows how things and people coproduce each other. Despite the desire for a world of ontological purity and nonhuman authenticity, things are a product of social relations and affect them at the same time. So, if things are caught up in myriad networks and relations and if they can be framed and used in any number of different ways, what does it mean to reframe rubbish?

As Thompson has shown it means a lot in terms of economies of value because of waste's crucial role in generating change. But what does it mean for person-thing relations? What triggers a reframing of rubbish, and what inhibits this? If you looked at examples from environmental education you'd assume that all it took was the voice of abstract moral reason, a television ad instructing you to "think again before you throw that out!" Many of these campaigns take a very simplistic approach to our material habitus and how it might be transformed. They tend to ignore how blind we can be to the everyday materiality of objects, how much we can take their instrumentality for granted, and how this blindness is enhanced when we seek to get rid of things. After all, disposal is a kind of purification ritual that restores us to an ordered state; that is its function and its pleasure. Framing things as rubbish doesn't just help us eliminate things from our lives; it also helps us experience the fantasy of self-sovereignty and ontological separateness. In order to be able to reject we have to convert objects into worthless rubbish simply meeting its fate. As one of our most everyday habits, disposal depends on a particular kind of blindness that helps us *not* see, *not* acknowledge the things we want to be free of. To throw things away is to subordinate objects to human action, it is to construct a world in which we think we have dominion. This doesn't just deny the persistent force of objects as material presence, it also denies the ways in which we stay enmeshed with rubbishy things whether we like it or not.

So, for rubbish to be framed differently it needs first of all to be *noticed*, it has to be become conspicuous. Before other possibilities and potentials emerge, before other games of value and use are activated, the phenomenological reality of rubbish has to be acknowledged. We have to recognize discarded objects not as the passive and redundant context for our lives but as mobile, vital matter open to reconstitution.[25] One pathway toward this, as I've suggested, might be recognizing waste as things. As Brown argues, things become conspicuous when they are in a state of transition between one thing and another, when they are in the process of being reanimated and resignified.[26] Things are different from the material object world and its primary circuits of exchange. They are what's left after objectification breaks down, they are what we suddenly notice when an object seems to drop out of all the systems that give it meaning and value. The tattered sofa on the sidewalk sitting there for days on end awaiting the garbage pickup captures our attention as a thing. Not quite waste yet and definitely out of place, it's just quietly biding its time. Its role in intimate, private lives lingers in the coffee stains on the arms, the permanent slump in the cushions, the secrets it's overhead. Its movement from the living room to the street, from useful to discarded, defamiliarizes it, putting us into a different relationship with it. Its sensuous physicality beckons, you feel like sitting in it as if for the first time.

Following Brown then, it may be the very thingness of rubbish that can save it from abandonment and that can move it into another system of value or allow us to imagine a new objectification for it. Irregularities of exchange and transitional states make thingness visible. Waste is often found in these situations, out of place, on the edges of order, ephemeral and phenomenal. Rethinking waste means rethinking all the practices that blind us to the reality and possibilities of what remains. This is the ethico-political challenge of waste: imagining a new materialism that would transform our relations with the things that we pretend not to see. But we don't have to imagine this from scratch. Agnes Varda's exploration of gleaning shows us how waste is reimagined and reused with great insight and pleasure.

GLEANING

Varda's film *The Gleaners and I* is a waste road movie. At the age of seventy-two this leading figure of French new wave cinema took to the road with a digital camera and collected a series of stories about different ways of living with waste. Part documentary on gleaning and contemporary practices of scavenging in France and part reverie on aging, Varda's film is an extraordinary visual essay on wasted and used things and their ethical force. The film is more than just a story of those living on the margins of excess and affluence, it is also a story of objects and their capacity for constant reclassification. Varda's achievement is to open up the question of person-thing relations in such a way that we are able to see the complexities of a different and radical ethics of waste at work. She does this *not* through moral lesson but through a cinematic technique that celebrates the camera's capacity to glean and the filmmaker's capacity to play with images and stories, to digress, to engage in reverie. Varda calls this *cinécriture*, a kind of "filmic writing."[27] The effect is a series of ethical and aesthetic speculations on waste that is moving and unsettling rather than dogmatic and hectoring. Watching this film we are not being instructed to reform our practices or pity those who live off waste. Rather, we are invited to experience a kind of intimacy and enchantment with the sensuousness of rubbish as things and to witness moments of conversion in which new use values are found for waste.

The value of *The Gleaners and I* for thinking about a new materialism lies in the way this film documents how people become responsive to waste and open to its possibilities. Through interviews and conversations Varda gives us remarkable access to the various ethico-political justifications people have for gleaning. By inviting people to talk about how they glean, where they do it, and why, she enables us to see the different kinds of recognition people have for waste; what makes them notice it, and what makes them imagine new relations with it. This is more than just the discovery of new uses for discarded things. It is also an exploration of how the creation of use values can be infused with ethical impulses. Gleaning becomes a way of translating a moral unease about excess or an ethic of self-sufficiency and survival into a specific set of material practices and habits. It also becomes a way of staying alive. Desperate need is the most compelling motivation for gleaning, and Varda explores it in depth. Consider the potato sequence.

Driving to the potato fields of Beauce in northern France, Varda ponders the reality of contemporary gleaning. While women did it in groups during the nineteenth century, as captured in Millet's famous painting "The Gleaners" (an image Varda cites as an inspiration for her film), now it is often a solitary practice, and men have taken it up. In a landscape of furrowed earth where an enormous commercial potato crop has just been harvested Varda talks to men stooping and searching for potatoes the grubbing machine has missed. They describe the best times and places to glean, foods to go with potatoes, restaurants they sometimes sell to. They also discuss their relationships with farmers, most of whom are happy to have gleaners clean the fields after harvest because of the savings in labor and chemicals.

The film then cuts to interviews with producers who talk straight to camera about the demands of the market, the restrictions supermarkets place on potato size and shape. What we are hearing is a description of the logic of seriality, the ways in which the commodification of food generates a very restricted set of requirements for what counts as a saleable potato. These restrictions lead to twenty-five tons of potatoes being dumped after each harvest in Beauce. We see the reality of this: trucks on the edges of fields emptying out load after load of edible potatoes. Standing around are people with bags ready to glean. A farmer reflects on the importance of the potato as a staple food and says that with the increase in dumping there has been an increase in gleaning. But at other dump sites there are no gleaners. After all, as Varda remarks, you never see a notice about the time and date of dumping in the local newspaper. People find out by word of mouth or observation, and this erratic and informal system means that thousands of potatoes go to waste. The camera pans over a landscape of rotting potatoes green with decay, dangerous to eat—the mortification of matter.

All these potatoes, all these different relationships with them; initially, Varda explores the human framing of the potato as a crop, as something to be sold or gleaned. The emphasis is on how diverse human actions manipulate and subordinate the potato to various systems of exchange. For the farmer the potato is a source of profit, for the gleaner it's a free source of food or something to barter with. Various talking heads tell a story about commodity cultures and the dynamics of different regimes of value. The effect isn't ethnographic; Varda avoids exoticizing gleaning and gleaners with an insistent focus on contexts and economic relations. The film shows how objects mediate social relations and how human interests shape different forms of appropriation: making money, surviving on social security. We could think about this as a kind of cinematic biography of potatoes, an account of their career as material, exchangeable objects—and an account of the different status they confer on people. But then there is a moment when this logic is disrupted, when Varda suddenly notices the thingness of one potato, when she is struck by its material self-evidence.

She's filming a man sorting through a big pile of dumped potatoes. As he discusses their remarkable shapes he encounters a heart-shaped one. Varda is surprised and delighted; she reaches out for it, struck by its phenomenology; its texture and shape captivate her. She attempts an awkward close-up, holding the potato in one hand and the digicam in the other. She then starts scrabbling through the pile looking for more. Cut to a table in Varda's apartment covered in heart-shaped potatoes. The camera explores them in close-up, moving sensuously over their surfaces, tracing the blotches on their skin. It's extraordinarily tactile. The camera brings the materiality of the potato into play—we don't just see the potatoes, we *feel* their dirt and bumps, they seem alive and vital and provocative.[28]

What is going on in this shift from a cultural biography of potatoes as commodities to a startling cinematic rendering of potatoes as material presence? One minute we're hearing people talk about what they *do* with potatoes, the next we're gazing at a pile of potatoes on a table, feeling like we could reach into the screen and pick them up. Is this an effect of the representational techniques of cinema, the camera capturing the world, or has the material force of the thing captured the camera? This if a false opposition, as vigorous debate in film theory has shown; cinema has always been fascinated by objects, and it has always been able to do things with things.[29] It has always been able to move them from the backdrop of human action to central characters in the story. There is a distinct cinematic rendering of things that makes them alluring, mysterious, alive, phantasmatic, *and* strikingly real. But in *The Gleaners* the issue isn't so much cinematic techniques and referentiality, it is witnessing objects becoming things and the ethical implications of this. The power of the heart-shaped potato lies in the way Varda captures the pleasure of surprise. Her chance encounter with a potato produces a response that is suffused with delight in the self-evidence, or the "suchness," of the phenomenon. Suddenly the potato isn't waste, it isn't a discarded object on the edge of decay, it isn't a testament to the excesses of agribusiness—it's a sensuous, wondrous thing. It's what's left over after all those frames of recognition drop away.

This is surely a case of what Brown describes as objects asserting themselves as things. And, following his schema, it is also a case of a changed subject-object relation. In this scene Varda digresses from the role of gleaner of facts, she takes a detour from the journalistic documentation of waste practices. The heart-shaped potato draws her and the audience into another relation. As she searches for more potatoes she pushes the camera closer and closer until we see the close-up pan over the potatoes on the table. It's impossible not to become caught up in the affect of this scene. The links between the visual and the tactile are striking. We are looking at and touching the potatoes, we are perceiving their *texture*. And it's through this imbrication of touch and vision that we experience Varda's sensuous enchantment with the thing. Texture makes trouble for any notion of a disembodied spectator, it foregrounds the ways in which looking and feeling are interconnected. As Eve Sedgwick says, a "particular intimacy seems to subsist between textures and emotions"; touching and feeling go together; "touching" doesn't just mean cutaneous contact, it means being affected, being altered by feelings.[30]

Obviously, it's not just the phenomenological resonances of this scene that reorder our relations with waste, it is also the question of affect. Or, to put it in Sedgwick's terms, it is the ways phenomenology and affect are connected. When we encounter waste as things the affective energy that can accompany this, the sense of wonder or horror, can be the impulse for new relations: a motivation for a different ethics, a sudden inspiration for a new use. In Varda's case the heart -shaped potato triggers a metonymic play from the shape of the heart to charity to those working with the poor and marginalized. The film shifts registers back into documentary mode, and we watch a man discussing how he gleans potatoes to serve in a soup kitchen for the hungry. He talks quietly about being unemployed and wanting to do something useful with his time and about the outrage of good food being dumped while people starve. It's a lovely evocation of a moral framework and motivation that is underlaid with the earlier scene of the beautiful heart-shaped potatoes. To confront the reuse of dumped potatoes as an ethical imperative reverberates with all the associations of them as remarkable physical things. That humble vegetable has got all sorts of holds on us; it can propel us toward acts of generosity and care, entrance us with its beauty and feel. By exploring the multiplicity of ways in which we are mixed up with potatoes—as commodity, as waste, as gift, as things—Varda offers us another way of understanding the ethics of waste. Waste makes claims on us. Reducing waste is not simply a matter of the moral reform of the human, it is also about acknowledging that waste has a kind of agency; that it shares in some of the agency we ascribe only to ourselves.[31]

VARDA'S HANDS

If the surprise of the heart-shaped potato sequence is that it lets us see wasted objects as vital and alive, the surprise of the hand sequence is that it lets us see a living body as dead. In revealing potatoes as things *The Gleaners and I* inaugurates a different kind of vision that is not so much instrumental and objectifying as tactile and intersubjective. The subject-object relation is unsettled by the ways in which the heart-shaped potato scene, in its appeal to texture and contact, evokes the multisensory qualities of perception.[32] It works because we carry sense memories of touching potatoes, because our hands bear the traces of their feel. But in another sequence we see that hands bear the traces of death.

Later in the film Varda is playing around with her digicam, filming objects in her apartment. She talks about their provenance, the pleasure of living with things collected over time. Suddenly, the digicam captures her free hand, the one that has been pointing at different things. She pauses on it, does a close-up, talking with horror about its wrinkles, blotches, and lines.

The hand is severed from her body, it becomes a thing separate and alien. In the image of her hand Varda sees her own death—the lines, blotches, and wrinkles are evidence of death at work. The hand appears to us as lifeless and worn out; Varda pauses to mourn her own loss. In that surprise glimpse of her hand we see a body asserting itself as a thing.

The surprise of the hand is that the digicam captures it as already dead, it signals its imminent status as waste. The surprise of the potatoes is that they appear to us as alive. How can this be when the visual techniques in these scenes are so similar? Both involve the contingency of a sudden, unexpected revelation; both involve the intensity of a lingering close-up on skin; both reveal the links between phenomenology and affect. Perhaps the difference between the two scenes has to do with waste. In the potato scene a wasted object asserts itself as a vital thing, in the hand scene a living subject becomes dead matter. What both scenes capture is the instability of waste; wasted objects can be reanimated and brought back to life, living subjects will become waste. Things pass from one state to another; waste, like thingness, is not inherent in things, it's a latency, an effect of certain sorts of recognition. Both these scenes trigger those recognitions, they notice waste in ways that disrupt the boundaries between subject and object, human and nonhuman, useful and useless, dead and alive.

The effect of this is to open up a very different way of thinking about and living with waste. Moral instruction and mastery of the "waste problem" are not the intentions of this film. These two scenes give waste a recognition and potency that make it much more than the bad object of environmental destruction and capitalist excess. Instead, waste becomes a relation in which we sense the force of conversion and transience, of other possibilities emerging, of enchantment *and* disturbance. In waste we see imagination and ethics coinciding: "I wonder what you could do with this?"

Hands and potatoes perform this different recognition of waste well, but so too do the much straighter documentary sequences in the film, in which Varda resists any tendency toward dogmatism. Her interviews with gleaners all over France are suffused with an openness and respect. People talking about their scavenging practices are filmed with unfailing intelligence and tenderness. Men and women found scrounging in bins behind supermarkets or in fields aren't victimized or shamed. Their anonymity and poverty are challenged by a documentary technique suffused with generosity. Varda isn't calculating the moral effect of their stories, the gleaners are not being used to generate sympathy. They're simply telling stories about a different kind of material habitus, a different way of living with things. This way of living is tough; surviving on waste involves a lot of work stooping, searching, and sorting. There's no romance in it, but there is dignity, and Varda's careful documentation of the micropractices of gleaning, the legalities of it, and the ways of converting and sharing what's scavenged is a beautiful exploration of the ethic of making do.

MAKING DO

"Making do" is also the theme of *Bush Mechanics*, but in this documentary the focus is on the pleasure and creativity of this practice more than its ethical import. Made in 1998, the film explores the relationship to cars of a group of young Aboriginal men from the Yuendumu community in remote Australia. Funny, innovative, and full of self-parody, *Bush Mechanics* reveals a completely different set of car practices from those usually seen and celebrated on commercial TV. There are no high-speed chases here, no glossy celebrations of the car as commodity fetish—rather, a set of madcap adventures about driving in the desert in cars chronically on the verge of mechanical collapse. The main content comes from watching these "bush mechanics" solve a variety of technical problems using whatever they can lay their hands on. Punctured inner tubes are replaced with densely matted spinifex grass, brake fluid is made from laundry detergent mixed with water, replacement parts are found on abandoned wrecks that are part of the collective memory in remote desert spaces. All this is evidence of a playful inventiveness prompted not simply by need but also by a robust practical knowledge about various ways of keeping a car moving.[33]

While making do is akin to gleaning because it involves scavenging, the term also implies creative *re*use with whatever is at hand. Analyses of this practice, also known as *bricolage*, have been taken up in anthropology (particularly by Lévi-Strauss) and, later, in cultural studies. *Bricolage* describes the human capacity to imagine and create new uses and meanings for things. This process is more than just reclassification, it involves an active reappropriation of things in different contexts that not only produces new meanings but also reveals the social logic of imagination. The capacity to subvert or erase original meanings and make new uses shows that imagination isn't fanciful or an activity restricted to leisure or aesthetics, it's a field of everyday social practice. Michel de Certeau has shown how central the arts of making do are to daily life.[34] Rituals, habits, routines are all a product of adapting ways of doing things with the material resources available.

While no one would question the fact of everyday creativity, cultural studies accounts of bricolage have tended to overvalorize human actions at the expense of a more relational materiality. Human agency is seen as driving the practice of bricolage, often in the interest of creating an oppositional or resistant identity.[35] This has had the effect of making bricolage seem like an act of subversion rather than a quotidian practice driven by pragmatic need. It has also, implicitly, reinforced a sharp opposition between inanimate material and human bodies with consciousness and intention, able to do weird and wonderful things with things.

The question that *Bush Mechanics* raises is: What if we thought of bricolage not as human activity in the service of identity but as evidence of what Latour calls the "networked quality of things?"[36] This is how *Bush Mechanics* represents the arts of making do, and this is what makes it a wonderful exploration of the relations between rubbish, recognition, and reuse. In this film representations of practical ingenuity continually foreground the heterogeneity of things in the world and the fluidity of their classification; things are continually open to new uses and frames of understandings. This is a road movie in which the ontological separation between the humans and the car is flattened, in which distinctions between mechanical, organic, human, and technological get very mixed up. The narrative momentum in the film is triggered by constant car breakdowns and the desperate desire of the five Yuendumu men to make it into town. Keeping the car moving means finding immediate solutions to a series of increasingly tricky technical problems.

While this scenario sounds like the perfect setting for a celebration of indigenous ingenuity, the film avoids this easy, feel-good representation of difference. Instead, it explores the exchanges and relays between a technology that both organizes human action and is subject to human inscription and will. This is a very demanding car. Keeping it on the road involves a radical openness to the technical possibilities of anything and everything. Consider the flat tire sequence—there's no spare or jack, so another solution has to be found. The men collectively lift the car onto a jerry can so they take the wheel nuts off with a pair of pliers. They then head off into the surrounding desert scrub and pull out bunches of spinifex to stuff into the tire. This tough desert grass turns out to be a perfectly reasonable substitute for the punctured inner tube.

In another scene the men wander into the scrub searching for a car wreck they think is nearby. It could provide the spare part that they need to keep moving. What unfolds is an alternative perception of the place of rubbish in natural space. For the bush mechanics, car carcasses are perceived as part of the landscape. Incorporated into the meanings of country, they are understood as traces, and, like rocks and mountains, they remain always available for transformation. Car bodies, like all material and organic things, are regarded as transient. While Western eyes might view these wrecks with moral opprobrium, as evidence of a crude disregard for natural purity, in *Bush Mechanics* they signal the value of traces, of refusing to erase presence. Deborah Bird Rose explains Aboriginal rubbish practices in this way:

> My Aboriginal teachers in the Northern Territory rarely picked up after themselves, but more to the point they did not seek to erase themselves. When they go fishing they call out to the ancestors and Dreamings saying, "Give us food, the children are hungry, we got kids here!" When they get food, they cook it on the spot. The remains of the dinner camps tell the stories of how they went to that place and called out to country, and how the country fed them. The remains of people's action in country tell an implicit story of knowledgeable action: these people knew where they were, they knew how to get the food that is there in the country. The country responded to their presence by providing for them, and the remains are evidence of the reciprocity between country and people. *In contrast, my teachers held self-erasure to be the equivalent of sneaking around the country.*[37]

So rubbish isn't rubbish, it's a literal trace that is available for transformation. It is part of the network of tracks that register movement and tell of events. It is potentiality, it can transform people and people can transform it. In a later television series of *Bush Mechanics* Jack Jakamarra Ross, a Yuendumu elder, is filmed wandering in the bush. Suddenly he comes across a defunct engine block. He looks at it closely and says: "This motor grew us up, now it is lying here like a witness looking after us."[38] The moment catches the viewer by surprise—here is someone describing how a car engine brought him up. This is far more radical than the common tendency to anthropomorphize your car with a cute name. Jack Jakamarra's account of his relation to an abandoned engine describes how the technological thing has metamorphosed into an affective agent that continues to watch over him. The thing has exchanged properties with a caring parent.

It's possible to read this scene as evidence of the charming naïveté of indigenous cosmology, but that would involve a denial of its disturbing pleasure and its implications for the meaning of rubbish as nothing but useless matter. The scene is *enchanting*; it disrupts our confident sense of the order of things, of the boundaries between human and nonhuman. It frames rubbish not as polluting dead object but as part of the landscape capable of bearing witness and always available for transformation.

I am using Jane Bennett's notion of enchantment here. She argues that the experience of enchantment is often linked to material metamorphoses, and that crossings and admixtures reveal the possibilities of radical shifts in meaning and matter. More important is the capacity of material metamorphoses to reveal the instability of ontology. Enchantment, for Bennett, is much more than a spectatorial delight; it is a moment of potential ethical transformation. "My wager is that if you engage certain crossings under propitious conditions, you might find that their dynamism revivifies your wonder at life, their morphings inform your reflections upon freedom, their charm energizes your social conscience and their flexibility stretches your moral sense of the possible."[39]

Both *The Gleaners* and *Bush Mechanics* satisfy Bennett's stringent checklist for enchantment. These are dynamic, wondrous films full of the pleasures and possibilities of rubbish. They stretch our "moral sense of the possible," as Bennett says, not by a moralizing critique of capitalism's excess and the burdens of waste, but by exploring the implications of framing rubbish differently. They energize our social conscience by giving us a glimpse of what a different materialism looks like.

NOTES

1. Don DeLillo, *Underworld* (New York: Scribner, 1997), 184–85.

2. John Frow describes DeLillo's account of the waste industry as a form of gangster capitalism in "Invidious Distinction: Waste, Difference and Classy Stuff," in *Culture and Waste: The Creation and Destruction of Value*, ed. Gay Hawkins and Stephen Muecke (Lanham, MD: Rowman and Littlefield, 2002).

3. W. G. Sebald, *Austerlitz* (London: Penguin, 2001), 31.

4. See James Wood, "Black Noise," *New Republic* 217, no. 19 (1997), for an excellent review of *Underworld*.

5. Bill Brown, "How to Do Things with Things (A Toy Story)," *Critical Inquiry* 25 (Summer 1998): 935; see also his account of the trace in the same essay.

6. The term *phenomenological hermeneutics* comes from Susan Buck-Morss, *The Dialectics of Seeing* (Cambridge, MA: MIT Press, 1991), 3.

7. This is Stephen Meuke's point in "A Landscape of Variability," in *Uncertain Ground: Essays between Art and Nature*, ed. Nicholas Thomas (Sydney: Art Gallery of New South Wales, 1999).

8. Bill Brown, "Thing Theory," *Critical Inquiry* 28 (Autumn 2001): 4–5.

9. Brown, "Thing Theory," 5.

10. Bill Brown, *A Sense of Things* (Chicago: University of Chicago Press, 2003), 4–5.

11. Elizabeth Grosz, *Architecture from the Outside* (Cambridge, MA: MIT Press, 2001), 168–69.

12. Gavin Lucas, "Disposability and Dispossession in the Twentieth Century," *Journal of Material Culture* 7, no. 1 (2002): 5–22; Nicky Gregson and Louise Crewe, *Second Hand Cultures* (Oxford: Berg, 2003).

13. See for example Susan Strasser, *Waste and Want: A Social History of Trash* (New York: Metropolitan Books, 1999); William Rathje and Cullen Murphy, *Rubbish! The Archaeology of Garbage* (New York: Harper Collins, 2001).

14. Igor Kopytoff, "The Cultural Biography of Things: Commoditization as Process," in *The Social Life of Things*, ed. Arjun Appadurai (New York: Cambridge University Press, 1986), 90.

15. Gregson and Crewe, *Second Hand Cultures*, 115.

16. Lucas, "Disposability and Dispossession," 14–19.

17. Gregson and Crewe, *Second Hand Cultures*, 201.

18. Michael Thompson, *Rubbish Theory: The Creation and Destruction of Value* (Oxford: Oxford University Press, 1979).

19. Thompson, *Rubbish Theory*, 7.

20. Thompson, *Rubbish Theory*, 108–9.

21. Frow, *Invidious Distinction*, 34–36.

22. Frow, *Invidious Distinction*, 36.

23. Frow, *Invidious Distinction*, 36.

24. John Frow, "A Pebble, a Camera, a Man Who Turns into a Telegraph Pole," *Critical Inquiry* 28 (Autumn 2001): 275.

25. Jane Bennett, *The Enchantment of Modern Life* (Princeton, NJ: Princeton University Press, 2001), 99.

26. Brown, "How," 954.

27. Chris Darke, "Refuseniks," *Sight and Sound* 11, no. 1 (January 2001): 30–31.

28. For a lovely reading of this scene see Anne Rutherford, "The Poetics of a Potato," *Metro Magazine* 137 (2003): 126–31.

29. For a great exploration of cinematic things see Lesley Stern, "Paths That Wind through the Thicket of Things," *Critical Inquiry* 28 (Autumn 2001).

30. Eve Sedgwick, *Touching Feeling*, vol. 28 (Durham, NC: Duke, 2003).

31. Bennett, *Enchantment*, 99.

32. See Laura Marks, *The Skin of the Film* (Durham, NC: Duke, 2000).

33. See Georgine Clarsen, "Still Moving: Bush Mechanics in the Central Desert," *Australian Humanities Review*, March 2002, at www.lib.latrobe.edu.au/AHR/archive/Issue-March-2002/clarsen.html (accessed March 7 2002), for a great reading of this documentary.

34. Michel de Certeau, *The Practice of Everyday Life* (Berkeley and Los Angeles: University of California Press, 1984).

35. For an example of this see Dick Hebdidge, *Subculture: The Meaning of Style* (London: Methuen, 1979).

36. Bruno Latour, *We Have Never Been Modern* (Cambridge MA: Harvard University Press, 1993).

37. Deborah Bird Rose, "Decolonizing the Discourse of Environmental Knowledge in Settler Societies," in Hawkins and Muecke, *Culture and Waste*, 62 (my emphasis).

38. Quoted in Clarsen, "Still Moving," 4.

39. Bennett, *Enchantment*, 32.

5

Empty Bottles

In the realm of urban phenomenology waste is most often something we see or smell. How hard would it be, then, to think of it as a sound? Consider this everyday acoustic event. First there is the rumble of a heavy truck moving slowly and erratically down a suburban street. This is an out-of-place rumble; trucks belong on arterial roads, not on quiet back streets—except, that is, for one morning each week. Then there is the sound of a bin being picked up, raised, and emptied into the truck, accompanied by the squeeze of a compressor packing the rubbish in, making room for the next load. A few minutes later another truck rumbles down the street, this time accompanied by the sounds of running feet, the odd phrase or joke yelled out, the human and the mechanical intermingling. Then there is the thud of newspapers landing on top of a pile and, finally, the crescendo, the crash of breaking glass, the sound of bottles disintegrating, being transformed from empty object into pure waste—*the end*.

But is it? Is the sound of breaking glass the sound of absolute loss and the destruction of value? In the era of recycling the idea of the end of value is hard to sustain. That crash is quite possibly the sound of a shifting register of value, a *beginning*, not an ending. Disintegration is not the moment when bottles die but the moment when they are reborn into the recycling economy and commence their transformation into "new" glass. The garbage truck isn't a site of desecration but an arena for the renegotiation and transformation of value. It's an economy on wheels that reminds us that waste can be commodified.

Consider also the reception of that sound, its cultural and affective meanings. How is it experienced by the people who have put those bottles on the curb? They might be lying in bed drowsy, and that crash, over and above all the other noises in the waste soundscape, might give them a little moment of satisfaction and well-being. As Mary Douglas shows us, garbage is pleasurable; the habits of cleansing and expelling do great service to identity. They make us feel momentarily whole. The boundary between me and not me is absolutely clear: "Rituals of purity and impurity create unity in experience. . . . They are positive contributions to atonement."[1] The binaries of self-waste and clean-dirty seem absolutely stable. The crash of the glass is a moment of closure that makes these oppositions seem inviolable.[2]

But is the pleasure in that sound simply a result of a successful purification ritual, or is it also connected to the experience of virtue? As I argue in chapter 2, recycling gives waste practices a moral dimension. After all, the journey of those bottles from the house to the garbage truck was complex and convoluted. Beyond the act of consumption were all those other little practices of classification and management that waste habits now involve. The pleasure in the moment of disintegration is the pleasure of the virtuous self, the pleasure of having been "a good sort" and done your bit for the environment, the pleasure of obedience to a moral rule.

Thinking about the resonances of this rubbish soundscape reveals the complex relations between waste and economy. While waste is often seen as the end or zero sum of value, as the uselessness that sustains utility, this denies waste's crucial role in the dynamics of value. The previous chapter shows how gleaning and making do involve the recuperation of wasted things, the creation of new uses and values for them. It shows how waste is generative of changes in value. Recycling shows how wasted matter can be subjected to the laws of profit and exchange; how markets can be created that implicate waste in new calculations and transactions. Waste is big business; getting rid of it or turning it into a resource is evidence of the relentless drive to commodify. It is also evidence that value is not an intrinsic property of things; it is contingent, a product of interdependent and shifting variables.

But what shifting variables have changed empty bottles and old newspapers from rubbish into resources? What new relations and regimes of value have reframed this material as residual commodity? It is impossible to answer this question in purely financial terms. In this chapter I argue that the process of enterprising waste that recycling reveals is also a process of enterprising the self. The creation of a distinctive recycling economy involved the development of new markets and manufacturing processes, new ways of relating to domestic rubbish, new identities for the waste-making subject—I'm a recycler!—and new problematizations of the place of waste in the environment. Money *and* meanings were involved, and their complex interconnections reveal the ways in which economies are just as much cultural as they are monetary. Recycling makes profits and new forms of subjectivity.

Recycling makes certain demands on subjects. Accepting these demands necessarily involves the calculation of benefits for the waste-making subject. As the experience of the sound of breaking glass reveals, recycling can make you feel good. Putting out the garbage now involves heterogeneous rules, practices, and calculations that produce a particular person. Presenting their rubbish on the street neatly sorted confers status on dutiful recyclers; it locates them in a social category, "responsible waste managers." The ensemble of norms, rules, and techniques that now surround waste management have made it into a form of self-actualization. Who could forget Kathleen Turner, playing the perfect middle-class mother in the film *Serial Mom*, turning on her neighbor on garbage night and declaring with self-righteous horror, "You mean you don't recycle?" Your waste and what you do with it can be a source of cultural capital or moral condemnation.

Recycling, then, is a good example of the fact of *multiple* economies—monetary, personal, and moral—and the complex transactions between them. The privileging of financial meanings for *economy* collapses in the face of evidence that cultural processes also function according to the logic of costs and benefits; and that "the economy" is as much a cultural site as, for example, a family or a school. The notion of economy applies to *any* dynamic structure that involves processes of exchange, circulation, and interested negotiation that are oriented toward some sort of goal, not necessarily gain.[3] How, then, does recycling reveal the interactions between commercial discourses on waste and calculations of personal and environmental value? Is it possible to maintain a dualism between the economics of recycling and its cultural and ethical meanings, to presume that the economic and the symbolic operate in separate and discrete spheres?

In this chapter I argue that it isn't possible to maintain such a dualism. My aim is to explore the "cultural economy" of recycling. This approach allows us to see that the process of enterprising waste, of turning it into a resource, was not exclusively economic. It was also cultural. Many analyses of the value of recycling focus on narrow cost-benefit assessments that derive from technical economics. Rather than assuming that this type of calculation neutrally evaluates an independent object, "the recycling industry," I argue that it functions as a discourse. Discursive practices produce their own object, they generate the forms of representation that allow economic action to be formatted and framed. By investigating the emergence of governmental and environmental discourses on recycling it is possible to see how this economy was constituted; how it generated a range of distinct material cultural activities, from separate bins to global markets in recycled goods; and how it was implicated in new styles of personal conduct. Recycling could not have taken off without substantial changes in the ways people related to their rubbish. The creation of markets in used paper or empty bottles, for example, depended on a discursive *re*framing of this type of waste at its point of production, the household, and concomitant shifts in domestic practices and waste management. Thinking about recycling as a distinct "cultural economy" presumes that the economic is an assemblage of contingent forces that are not simply monetary. It allows us to track how wasted material was turned into economic objects and how particular persons were produced not only to prepare this material for recirculation back to industry but also to purchase the products that resulted from it.

John Law offers a useful tool kit for assessing the dynamics of cultural economies. He insists that all economic activity is cultural in a broad sense.[4] Rather than seeing culture as the other of economy, as the realm of beliefs and symbols or the zone of nonutilitarian symbolic order, he argues that economic activity is a set of material practices produced by certain techniques and discourses. Following this, economies need to be understood as materially heterogeneous relations involving practices, subjects, and distinct "cultures" that include specific techniques of calculation. These relations are performed and are therefore subject to constant variation. Law writes:

Markets, then, or economics . . . involve performing calculations, monetary exchanges, transactions and relations of all kinds. But what does this take in practice? Any answer to this question becomes an investigation of practice. It becomes an investigation of the ordering of materially heterogeneous socio-technical economically relevant relations, their enactment and performance. It also becomes an investigation of the constitution of relevant forms of agency and subjectivity.[5]

Using this concept of cultural economy I want to investigate practices of recycling in terms of how they organize relations and transactions between waste and subjects. How was recycling invented, and what types of rationalities and calculations of value were developed to market this practice to populations? How was the subjectivity "recycler" produced? And how was the rise of recycling implicated in wider cultures of consumption and an ethos of disposability? What this approach to recycling shows is that it is impossible to sustain any kind of distinction between practices that are seen as intrinsically meaningful, as the realm of culture is so often represented, and those driven by the logic of instrumental reason, the typical domain of the economic. More significantly, the rise of recycling shows that the pursuit of rationalized economic objectives for enterprising waste was utterly reliant on the development of new trainings and disciplines in households. That is: it relied on the development of a new set of ethical goals for waste management that constituted recycling as a domain of virtue and recyclers as virtuous. In enterprising waste, the creation of new economic and ethical values for discarded matter was an interdependent process.

In order to understand recycling as a cultural economy I begin with some history: How did contemporary recycling become thinkable? When the rise of recycling in the 1960s is compared with practices of reuse in the nineteenth century, it is possible to see how the recent reinvention of recycling involved the creation of a very different cultural economy. In the nineteenth century waste wasn't enterprised in the name of environmental protection or concern for the planet. It was part of a complex network of transactions between burgeoning industry, household cultures of reuse and scarcity, and underdeveloped governmental systems of removal.

But history gets you only so far. Analyzing two current techniques for calculating the value of recycling—cost-benefit analyses and qualitative evaluations of people's attachments to this practice—makes it possible to see that economic and ethical value are not antagonistic. They often involve the same methodology but mobilize different discourses of value to defend their assessments.

However, while analyses of recycling as a cultural economy are good for understanding *how* this practice works, this descriptive methodology is less useful for assessing the ethico-political impacts of recycling. By shifting focus from the idea of cultural economy to that of gift economy I take up critiques of recycling by some environmentalists. Is recycling a ruse, a sap to middle-class guilt, as some claim, or is it evidence of a complex gift economy? Unlike those who reject recycling as making little difference to the state of the environment, I focus, in the terms of my assessment, on the ethics of generosity. Is recycling an obligation or a magnanimous gesture? Whose interests are served by it, and whose are ignored? And could the distinctive set of sociotechnical relations that it generates contain the possibility of a more sustainable ethics of waste?

REINVENTING RECYCLING

Claims about the novelty and value of recycling are sometimes met with derision. For those old enough to remember life before excessive consumption, recycling and reuse were, and still are, unremarkable practices—part of the way in which scarcity is managed and the life of things extended. It is also an ethos that constitutes the careful reuser as an efficient and diligent household manager: waste not, want not. Susan Strasser calls this culture of reuse the "stewardship of objects" and links it to a range of historical factors.[6] Prior to the emergence of mass consumption in the late nineteenth century and the ethos of disposability that I document in chapter 2, people had greater investments in the objects they used. They had an awareness of the labor involved in making objects, they had skills in creating new uses for objects, and they were actively involved in realizing potential and ongoing use value. Darning socks, sewing rags into rugs, using tea leaves to clean carpets, and using old clothes to make new ones are some of the myriad examples Strasser documents to show how time, labor, and inventiveness underpinned a widespread culture of reuse. The absence of organized state-managed rubbish collection was also a factor. Rubbish was a household problem, something to be dealt with on-site, not handed over to public authorities.

The growth of early manufacturing saw techniques of reuse extended into wider spheres. Strasser's analysis of this development locates recycling at the heart of early industry. Rag and bone collectors established direct links between households and factories, taking household wastes back to factories for conversion into products. Wholesalers, peddlers, and storekeepers became waste middlemen, buying waste materials from households, then sorting and baling them for resale to industry. Those short of cash could still participate in the nascent consumer economy by getting credit for valuable wastes and exchanging them for new things.

This account of the rise of manufacturing documents the interdependence between household and factory in terms of the circulation of waste and goods. Strasser says, "Materials literally cycled between households and factories, creating a *two-way* relationship between manufacturers and consumers."[7] Moreover, she shows how an existing culture of reuse in households made the development of certain industries and forms of consumption possible. Households grounded in habits of reuse and conservation had materials readily available for the factories that depended on them; they were also entirely open to the purchase of new things made from old.[8]

Strasser's history of nineteenth-century waste practices reveals a recycling economy at work long before the reinvention of this term in the 1960s. She shows how waste circulated as a currency in the rise of the factory and how a myriad of diverse systems of exchange from barter to peddling allowed all sorts of people to enterprise waste and extract maximum value from it. Gradually these systems of exchange dispersed, and informal economies were marginalized by the rise of specialized waste dealers and wholesalers who began to dominate the trade in waste. Household wastes became devalued in this process as new and cheaper raw materials were found to substitute for them. Beyond this, the gradual expansion of consumption and mass markets meant that buying new began to acquire status and become a marker of class distinction. The ability to dispose of things without concern, to make waste, was a sign of wealth, and in this way getting rid of things was separated from production, consumption, and use.[9]

This brief history provides an important context for analyses of contemporary recycling. It shows that the forms of reuse and recirculation of waste practiced in the nineteenth and early twentieth century, while prefiguring current practice, were also distinctly different. They did not emerge out of social activism or mass public education, they did not involve representations of nature in crisis, and they did not involve a radical reframing of domestic habits and values. My point is not that earlier versions of recycling are more authentic. Rather, they involved the enactment of a specific cultural economy that exploited and enhanced already existing networks between waste materials, emergent industry, and household practices. The assemblage of sociotechnical relations that constituted nineteenth-century recycling involved the performance of different practices and different calculations of value and subjectivity.

The reinvention of recycling in the 1960s was a product of quite different forces. It involved a diverse set of discourses and techniques that had to be disseminated, stabilized, and implanted in practices of various kinds from the governmental to the domestic. Tracking these forces illuminates how rubbish became an object of new economic relations and recycling a source of ethical self-improvement. While current recycling involves similar movements of waste from homes back to industry, the personal meanings of this practice, how its value is calculated, the business and government organizations that are involved, and the rationalities that justify it mean that the way we recycle now is a vastly different practice from its antecedents. We are dealing with another cultural economy altogether.

A thorough-going genealogy of recycling is not my aim. Rather, I want to deploy a set of loosely genealogical methods to track how contemporary recycling became thinkable, and in what ways it connected a set of cultural and social objectives about domestic waste practices to the recovery of commodity value in rubbish. I'm concerned, here, with sketching discursive shifts, with exploring how language and ideas capture and construct events. Three broad shifts were crucial to the reinvention of recycling: the rise of an environmental movement that problematized nature, debates about the effects of excessive consumption, and shifts in the economics of the waste management industry prompted by the governmental discovery of "the waste crisis."

Most accounts of the reinvention of recycling cite the rise of environmental movements as crucial. In the 1960s environmentalists began protesting about the excesses of rapid capital expansion evident in belching smokestacks, contaminated waterways, and increasingly visible urban waste. Initially, the target of this discourse was industry. Industrial pollution was seen as the main cause of ecological destruction, and this is why factories and their filthy byproducts featured heavily in apocalyptic accounts of nature under siege. This emergent concern for "the environment" framed nature as passive and vulnerable to gross exploitation by rampaging capital. The political effects of this movement were the development of an increased regulatory framework for industry, evident in the rise of antipollution and other environmental laws in most capitalist democracies; the creation of specific bureaucracies such as environmental protection agencies; and a range of other legislative initiatives and reforms that acted to safeguard nature. This representation of human activity destroying nonhuman nature is classically modernist. As Ghosh and Muecke argue, it puts man at the center of the story surrounded by an "environment," and it perpetuates the idea of a fundamental opposition between nature and culture.[10] Rather than framing the human and nonhuman relation in terms of interconnection, early environmentalism privileged notions of protection.

Paralleling the rise of environmentalism was a less prominent discourse about cultures of consumption and the problem of abundance. Vance Packard's 1963 widely read classic, *The Waste Makers*, is often cited as the key source of this critique.[11] Packard's polemic exposed consumption practices to sweeping moral critique.[12] American consumers were buying too much. They had been seduced by the cult of the new and were victims of the planned obsolescence of industry, which trapped them in a treadmill of disposability. Their values were being eroded by the rise of freely available credit that fuelled the pressure to consume. Hedonism and the effects of material abundance, evident in the incredible glut of things in homes, were producing a population that lacked restraint and prudence and found satisfaction in self-indulgent, conspicuous consumption.

While environmentalism was concerned with the state of nature, Packard was concerned with the state of the "average citizen of the United States." His book pursues the question: "What is the impact of all this pressure towards wastefulness on the United States and on the behavior and character of its people?"[13] This focus on character, on the kind of ethos and sensibility that overconsumption produces, establishes a very different connection between practices of self-fulfillment and shopping. While the discourses of consumer sovereignty represented shoppers in a state of permanent and occasionally ecstatic self-actualization, Packard saw most consumption as fundamentally wasteful: unnecessary, frivolous, and offering false satisfaction. Although he was scathing in his attack on business practices and the ways in which industry's demands for economic growth advocated waste, his primary focus was the moral decline of the citizen shopper.

What this argument did was constitute the household and domestic habits as a field open to action. Packard's recommendations for change and reform advocated a range of practices aimed at helping consumers "regain a posture of self-respect in the shopping situation."[14] Rejecting products that favored fashion over function, developing techniques of prudence and restraint, doing volunteer work rather than going to the mall, and ignoring advertising were all seen as restoring the psychological health of the shopper and giving him or her a sense of pride and dignity.

Packard's argument was moralistic and nostalgic, but its wider resonances were important. In criticizing consumption practices and household habits he prefigured the emergence in the mid-1960s of not only consumer rights but also consumer responsibility. His representation of consumers was ambiguous; they were both the victims of gross manipulation by big business and activist subjects who could and should take steps in their everyday lives to resist the rise of wastefulness and disposable culture. Shopping became infused with guilt, and shoppers became open to reform and improvement, with the development of a new conscience and lifestyle.

The final discursive shift necessary to the reinvention of recycling was the construction of a waste crisis. This was partially an effect of environmentalism, which had consistently used images of mountains of waste to push its message. It was also a result of shifts in governmental practices around waste and pressures on the economics of the waste industry. The complex intersections of these forces led to the identification of the "waste problem." While versions of this story vary according to different locales and political structures, the basic plot remains the same. From the late 1970s governments at all levels began noting the increasing costs of waste removal and disposal. Waste has always been a major infrastructure cost for public administration, but by the 1970s growing amounts of waste and the decline in suitable landfill sites began to generate shifts in how waste was framed as a governmental issue. Technocratic discourses about waste that focused on how to get rid of it fast and cheaply were displaced by new approaches that problematized waste as a worrying cause of spiraling government cost blowouts and environmental degradation.

Waste was no longer the exclusive object of engineering and the transport industry; it was now configured as a problem of *how we lived*. Consider, for example, this opening sentence of a government report on waste from the early 1980s: "Australians are among the world's largest generators of municipal solid waste on a per capita basis and this reflects our life style and high standard of living."[15] Here, the source of excessive waste is shifted from industry to the household and "lifestyle." In the same report waste is also represented as an unexploited resource, as an unacceptable burden on the environment, and as part of that amorphous network described as *civic responsibility*. The effect of these new governmental discourses was the gradual replacement of *disposal* with *management*. The emergence of terms like *minimization, audits, sustainability*, and *recycling* constituted waste as something to be "managed" in the interests of industry efficiency and environmental care. This generated substantial transformations across all levels of social and economic administration, from the macrolevel of legislative change to the microlevel of the household. The question is, *how* did household practices become implicated in wider reforms of waste management? And how were these transformations experienced in everyday life? What reordering of personal habits and relations to rubbish emerged as a result?

The widespread implementation of curbside recycling programs in late capitalist countries from the 1970s is generally seen as the touchstone of the shift from thoughtless disposal to careful management. It is also one of the most significant changes in personal conducts around rubbish in the late twentieth century. The diverse discursive, political, and economic forces that underpinned this change produced a new network of socio-technical relations around some sorts of waste, how it was managed in households, how it was collected, and what became of it after pickup.

The normalization of recycling could not have happened without the convergence of three crucial ideas that made it thinkable: environmental crisis, living responsibly, and rubbish as a resource. Each of these ideas was central to promoting recycling, to putting householders into new relations with their rubbish, and to showing subjects how the performance of certain actions would make them into virtuous "recyclers." In different ways these ideas formed the distinct set of calculations of benefit that the implementation of recycling depended on. Households may have had little choice in changing their rubbish practices, but the extent of the take-up of recycling, the sense in which populations willingly embraced it, willingly acted on themselves, is evidence that more than coercion or discipline was at stake.[16] Recycling policies linked processes of subjectivity and self-actualization with wider governmental reforms in waste administration. As a political technology these policies and programs established a connection between the state of the environment, personal practices, and economic benefit.

The reinvention of recycling from the 1970s onward involved a set of meanings and practices very different from those of its antecedents. The calculations of its benefits were inextricably linked to the concept of "nature" as an abstract singular space in need of care and protection. As I've argued, this conceptualization of nature is relatively recent, a product of the rise of political ecology and environmentalism. What recycling did was shift the focus of environmentalism from industry and production to households and consumption. It personalized rhetorics of global environmental degradation by implicating everyday practices like shopping and putting out the garbage. These were now part of the problem, and recycling was a way of making them part of the solution. "Acting locally," as in changing your household habits, aligned reform of the self with global environmental good.

Nature under threat situated contemporary recycling in a new set of moral and economic relations. It expanded the ethical claims of this practice way beyond an ethos for living prudently. While household practices were fundamental to nineteenth-century forms of recycling, the targeting of households from the 1970s on was based on a very different set of rationales. Contemporary householders do not seek to enterprise their waste, to use it to enhance income or to barter for goods; they get no economic returns for recycling. Householders' actions go unrewarded *except* in ethical terms. The money is made higher up, when local government or recycling collection companies sell the materials that have been voluntarily sorted by householders. In the contemporary cultural economy of recycling there are diverse calculations of its benefit: ethical, environmental, and economic. And it is the tensions between these different measures of value that feature in debates over whether recycling is actually worth it.

CALCULATING THE BENEFITS OF RECYCLING

In 1996 the *New York Times Magazine* published an article by John Tierney titled "Recycling Is Garbage."[17] In it Tierney rails against the fervor for recycling. He accuses Americans of being racked with "garbage guilt" and supporting an activity that is basically inefficient and wasteful:

> Recycling does sometimes make sense—for some materials in some places at some times. But the simplest and cheapest option is usually to bury garbage in an environmentally safe landfill. . . . Mandatory recycling programs aren't good

for posterity. They offer mainly short-term benefits to a few groups—politicians, public relations consultants, environmental organizations, waste-handling corporations. . . . Recycling may be the most wasteful activity in modern America: a waste of time and money, a waste of human and natural resources.[18]

Tierney's critique challenges every claimed benefit of recycling, from environmental improvement to cost saving. By his calculations recycling is economically irrational. The costs of administering household collection programs far outweigh the profits to be gained from the reuse of waste and the benefits to nature. The money spent on maintaining a massive recycling apparatus would be much better allocated to schools and welfare.

Tierney's argument has plenty of shock value. In challenging the accepted benefits of recycling he privileges economic efficiency as the best technique for evaluating waste management. Despite all the fuss, however, this critique is nothing new. Since the reinvention of recycling there have been continual debates over its value. The rise of recycling has spawned a massive array of social technologies—from evaluation, to focus groups, to economic impacts modeling—all aimed at capturing and assessing its costs and benefits. The mountain of reports and facts and figures produced both represent recycling and make it available to different sorts of calculative agency. This diverse and contradictory knowledge of recycling is used, for example, by governments to justify changes in waste collection, by environmental groups in various campaigns, by advertising agencies in the social marketing of recycling. This knowledge becomes active in the production, performance, and ordering of a multiplicity of relations and activities that constitute recycling as a material practice. In seeking to analyze the benefits of recycling the issue is not which technique of evaluation is right or wrong, which gets closest to the "real" cost of recycling. Rather, we should investigate what measures of value various assessments of recycling deploy, and what sorts of calculative agency they produce, particularly for the domestic recycler.

Many assessments of recycling begin with a discussion of the dangers of *over*valuing this activity. A common representation is of a waste management apparatus that is enormously cumbersome, in terms of both collection and reconstitution, that *feels good but costs a fortune*. Echoing Tierney, these assessments point to the difficulties in making "realistic" calculations in the light of inflated environmental claims and suspect emotions: "Even the most ardent supporters of recycling must accept that recycling is not a panacea for our environmental problems, nor should it be pursued to the point of diminishing returns or at any cost."[19]

This approach deploys cost-benefit analysis, a technique that frames "benefit" in terms of efficient arrival at a specifiable bottom line that is generally monetary. The calculative logic of this technique is derived from economic measurements that seek to asses whether the costs of collecting, transporting, storing, cleaning, and developing special manufacturing techniques to use recyclable wastes are outweighed by the profits that are made selling them. This sort of calculation is what Barbara Herrnstein Smith terms "classic utilitarianism"; it links measures of economic value to technical notions of efficiency, practicality, and instrumentality.[20] It also establishes utility as a pure good and seeks to exclude any nonutilitarian variables as irrelevant and contaminating.

The second form of calculation that recycling has been subjected to measures all the risks and benefits that the first model resolutely excludes as *incalculable*; all those heterogeneous and subtle measures of value like "community benefit," "environmental impacts," and "consumer awareness." These are the measures classic utilitarianism rejects as resolutely "noneconomic." Smith defines this alternative and often marginalized form of calculation as "anti-utilitarian humanism."[21] And, despite the assumption that these two forms of calculation—the utilitarian and the humanist—are fundamentally antagonistic, part of the great divide between economy and culture, she contends that they are *not* fundamentally discontinuous. They both involve the same methodology, cost-benefit calculations, it is just that this technique is mobilized by different discourses of value and is defended and justified according to different interests. While classic utilitarianism assesses economic benefits in the interests of rationality and efficiency (i.e., specifically market-driven associations), antiutilitarian humanism defines benefit in terms of a range of cultural and symbolic variables in the interests of more diffuse values like protection of the environment, community involvement, or individual contribution.

In many assessments of recycling, however, these two techniques of evaluation are not opposed. They are combined to produce hybridized calculations in which the economic and the cultural are recognized as thoroughly enmeshed. Economic rationality is not seen as overriding other measures of value. Instead, economic processes are understood as interdependent with the cultural via a network of relations that make it difficult to identify clear distinctions between exploiting waste's potential as a resource and everyday social practices that seek to manage it with ethical concern.

An excellent example of this hybridized technique of calculation can be found in a 1990 report titled *Interim Report on Paper Recycling*. This seemingly innocuous report, one of many in the mountain of government documents on recycling, makes an extraordinary effort to measure and value the role of households and voluntary individualism in facilitating recycling. It argues that householders, through their time and effort, currently bear the primary cost of waste separation and sorting. This activity is fundamental to the operations of the recycling industry; without it recycling would not be economically feasible. The report acknowledges that the economic benefits of recycling depend on specific household practices voluntarily and willingly carried out by the population; and that this voluntary contribution has taken place in the face of steadily *increasing* charges for domestic waste removal.

In other words, there has been no economic incentive for householders to embrace the new classification and separation activities that recycling demands. Most are paying more for restricted waste services that involve more personal effort. How, then, do householders calculate the benefits of recycling? According to the report, most people surveyed saw the benefits of recycling as entirely *ethical*; they recycled because they were "motivated by a concern for the environment."[22] This report documents a widespread moral attachment to recycling and shows that it is impossible to reduce this waste practice to a purely economic logic. Instead, what is revealed is a network of practices and benefits that are heterogeneous and not entirely coherent. As an industry recycling can function only with the assistance of free labor from householders, this underpins its economic viability. But the people who perform this labor do not experience themselves as volunteer workers in the recycling industry. They do not generally assess their actions as economically relevant. Rather, in performing the actions of a "recycler" they think of themselves as doing something good for nature and the environment. They see themselves as performing ethical, not economic, work.

RECYCLING AS A PERFORMANCE

In recognizing the complex interconnections between economic and cultural processes this report on waste paper foregrounds the crucial role of everyday domestic actions in assessing the wider impacts of recycling. This emphasis on material practices in the home makes it possible to see how recycling is much more than a set of policies programmed into bodies, it is a distinct *performance*. Law argues that cultural and economic processes don't exist in the abstract, they have to be enacted. These enactments involve a set of heterogeneous elements, all of which are performing to produce certain relations, orderings, and calculations of value. Material practices extend beyond humans; they implicate technical, architectural, geographical, and corporeal arrangements.[23] Recyclers, then, are not active agents managing their passive waste; recyclers are part of a network of relations in which used newspapers and empty bottles, the containers they're put in, the trucks that pick them up, the companies that buy them, and the governmental and popular discourses that justify these actions all become vital elements in the performance of environmental good and a distinctive subjectivity. For the householder, the carefully sorted containers on the street are a gift to the environment that symbolically confers value on the person who placed them there. This value is both ethical and affective. Recycling makes many people feel good, this is the calculative benefit that motivates the repeated performance of sorting and rinsing, week after week. These actions don't just produce the subjectivity "recycler," they also connect this subject to "the environment," giving minor domestic actions an ethical resonance.

This way of arranging the elements of recycling and producing distinct calculations about its value is, however, entirely contingent. Strasser's analysis of the nineteenth-century history of reuse has already shown that. An account of recycling in Japan offers different evidence of how recycling can generate quite diverse modes of calculative agency and material semiotic relations. Sandra Buckley tells a fascinating story about Japanese recycling that shows how this practice become incorporated into wider networks of status and competition between housewives.[24] While waste reduction may have been the ostensible policy objective, in practice this goal was often displaced by the zealous desire to use recycling to display domestic skills and impress the neighbors.

In the 1980s the municipality of Otsu in the Osaka-Kyoto region introduced a new garbage disposal system aimed at streamlining collection and recycling. Households were issued five sets of colored garbage bags, each representing a different type of waste product: glass, metals, combustibles, plastics, and paper. Once these bags were filled with the correct waste matter, householders had to take them to a centralized collection point on the correct day of the week to be picked up. Each type of bag was picked up on a different day. Bags could not be left outside this collection point overnight. They were also labeled, on one side with detailed instructions on how to handle the waste matter before putting it in the bag, on the other with a slogan declaring allegiance to the "Movement for the Reduction of Volume of Refuse." Below this was a space where each household name was to be written. As Buckley says, "Each family was thus expected to own both its garbage and its performance as a member of the community."[25] Even when protests led to the removal of the space for the name of the household on bags, 80 percent of householders continued to write their names on the bags, keen to display their compliance with a new garbage regime.

This recycling apparatus was technically complex and time consuming, particularly for housewives. Discursively, its object was not so much the production of an environmentally concerned subject as the reduction of waste in the name of civic duty and obedience. This obedience was often overlaid with techniques that turned recycling into competitive display. Buckley describes how in other parts of Japan a company marketed clear garbage bags with enormous success. These bags gave housewives the chance to display their waste, in order

> to demonstrate not only the quality of their garbage but also their level of professionalization: perfectly peeled fruit skins, neatly compressed milk cartons, perfectly folded scraps of paper. One could also demonstrate the level of technological sophistication of the household—electronically opened cans, pre-shredded waste paper, cans compacted by an electronic crusher, assorted waste from brand name appliances. . . . Garbage is treated by the professional housewife as a serious opportunity to be judged by her peers.[26]

Buckley's account describes a very different way of drawing the elements of recycling together. The socio-technical effect of the see-through garbage bag is to make rubbish active in conferring status on the housewife. Food scraps and milk cartons, which are now visible, become agents in neighborhood relations and rivalry. Buckley's final assessment is that the emphasis on recycling as heightened public performance has had little impact on producing less rubbish in Japan. Instead, recycling has become an integral element of household ritual and neighborhood dynamics. The calculation of its value is linked not to concern for the environment but to conscientious domestic practice and the status and identity of the professional housewife. "Environmentalists trying to link local issues of waste disposal to global issues of deforestation describe a sense of frustration at the public resistance to translating these connections into action in everyday consumer practice."[27]

The case of Japan highlights how recycling as a cultural economy involves contingent and materially heterogeneous logics and relations. There are different styles of recycling, each generating distinct practices, subjectivities, and techniques for calculating the worth of this activity. Accepting this diversity, I am still troubled by the problem of how to assess it in more general political terms. I still want to pursue the question of whether recycling does or could make a difference to environmental decline.

FROM CULTURAL ECONOMIES TO GIFT ECONOMIES

While a cultural economy approach is useful for understanding *how* recycling works as a socio-technical arrangement, it offers few tools for judging recycling's political and environmental impacts. It has helped identify the particular techniques of calculation that are produced in different styles of recycling. But what to make of this? Is recycling good? What calculations could be mobilized to judge its effects, and what kind of critical consciousness could be brought to bear on it? These questions demand a different mode of analysis. They demand a shift from a largely descriptive analysis to a normative analysis. In making this shift I do not want to adopt the usual terms of critique set down in environmentalist rejections of recycling. Rather, I want to assess this activity as an example of a gift economy. This opens up other lines of analysis that allow us to consider in what ways recycling functions as a minor practice that, through the gesture of generosity, changes how we relate to waste. But how generous is recycling, and who benefits from its gifts?

Timothy Luke provides a good example of the standard environmentalist critique of recycling:

> In the ruse of recycling, green consumerism, rather than leading to the elimination of massive consumption and material waste, instead revalorizes the basic premises of material consumption and massive waste. By providing the symbolic and substantive means to rationalize resource use and cloak consumerism in the appearance of ecological activism, the cult of recycling as well as the call

to save the earth are not liberating nature from technological exploitation. On the contrary, they cushion, but do not end the destructive blows of an economy and a culture that thrive upon transforming the organic order of nature into the inorganic anarchy of capital.[28]

As passionate as this critique is, it is not the approach I want to take. While I agree with Luke's assessment that high-consumption Western lifestyles are unsustainable, I am uneasy with the effects of this familiar cultural narrative. The moralism and hectoring tone victimize nature as the passive other to human exploitation and the anarchy of capital, generating a sense of despair and cynicism. When the exploitative force of power is so overcoded, why bother contesting it? I am uncomfortable with this representation of recycling as another example of disenchantment and destruction. It leaves no space for any recognition of the sensibilities and ethical attachments recyclers may feel for this activity or for the role of ethical practice in change. For Luke, recycling is a ruse because recyclers are blind to the "real" impacts of their actions— though he, of course, isn't. If we accept this critique then we have to negate the evaluations recyclers make of their practices, we have to dismiss their ethical experience as nothing more than false consciousness.

In rejecting this approach I am not seeking to become an apologist for recycling, to suggest that tokenism is better than nothing. Rather, I want to develop another line of analysis that facilitates a critical and careful assessment of the ethico-political implications of recycling for social justice. I want to shift the terms of judgment from whether recycling is good for the environment to how it is experienced as "good" by recyclers. And in what ways is this goodness or ethical value transacted? As I've argued, many evaluations of recycling document a deep moral attachment to this practice, but what is the nature of this attachment? Could the voluntary work that constitutes household recycling function like a gift economy? If so, what is the nature of the gift and whose generosity is recognized?

In focusing on the social rather than environmental impacts of recycling I don't want to dismiss questions of ecological decline and the exploitation of nature. As Andrew Ross has argued, social and environmental justice are inextricably connected: "Resource shortages and ecological degradation are primarily a result of uneven social measures that manufacture scarcity all over the world for the economic and political gain of powerful interests."[29] Accepting this fundamental connection, what kinds of scarcity and exploitation are necessarily forgotten in the gesture of Western recycling, and how might this be challenged? What are the productive dimensions and possibilities of recycling? Could it be the basis for extended and transformed relations with nature, with commodities, and with those who have nothing to recycle?

The idea of the gift is a useful way to start pursuing these questions, for gifts foreground questions of generosity and the relations between those who give and those who receive. In many campaigns promoting recycling the practice is represented as a gift: "Be a good sort—the environment will thank you." The effort that is entailed is framed not in terms of coercion or compliance but as a *magnanimous gesture*. Generosity and concern for nature are seen to overrule self-interest. Recycling isn't a duty; it's a way of deliberately and carefully giving up your waste as a means to making the world better. These are the terms in which it is possible to think about recycling as a gift economy and to consider the nature of the generosity that underlies it.

Recent debates about the nature of the gift have focused on its "constitutive ambivalence."[30] This ambivalence centers on whether it is possible for the gift to escape the transaction of value, to be truly gratuitous and therefore outside the play of social interest. Most argue that it isn't, and while the bases of this assessment may differ, the effect is to render the gift impossible.[31] Gift economies are inevitably caught up in the logic of a social contract, a relation of obligation and reciprocity that means that generosity cannot escape the calculation of benefit: What's in it for me? This calculative role does not mean that generosity is without virtue or moral import, but it does limit the possibilities of the gift in certain ways.

Rosalyn Diprose's account of corporeal generosity opens up an important line of thinking beyond the existing aporia of the gift.[32] For Diprose, generosity is fundamental to the pursuit of sociality and social justice, but, in order for us to realize this, it has to be understood as more than an individual gesture and virtue. She begins with a careful elaboration of the limits of theories of generosity that frame it within the logic of a social contract. Generosity can be cultivated and habituated and can involve the deliberate choice to give beyond the call of duty. It can enhance the well-being of the recipient and give pleasure to the giver, but this relation can never escape an economy of exchange between sovereign individuals in which "virtue is the subject of calculation."[33]

Moreover, when one is obligated to give, when it becomes a duty, then generosity is not in play. In both these cases the capacity to give presumes a reflexive, separate individual whose choices are guided by careful deliberation. According to Diprose, generosity should not be reducible to an economy of exchange between sovereign individuals. This structuring of the gift can never contribute to social justice because, when the freedom to give is claimed, individual self-sovereignty and property ownership are seen as pregiven, as *coming before* generosity: "In claiming freedom and property as one's own, something has already been taken from others. The generosity of the individual property owner who gives his or her acquisitions . . . is built on the generosity of others."[34] In other words, some forms of generosity confer value and identity on the giver, but this is done at the expense of a certain forgetting, a denial of the gifts of others who are rendered invisible or less worthy.

Diprose's critique makes trouble for the idea of recycling as a gift in several important ways. First, it shows that the logic of duty and obligation that people may feel in relation to this practice undercuts the possibility of generosity. Resentment would seem a much more likely response. Second, even those who document an experience of ethical satisfaction in recycling, who find pleasure in giving to the environment, cannot escape an exchange relation. In return for the cultivation of careful habits they enhance their identity as virtuous. And finally, the capacity to recycle, to give away not just waste materials like paper and glass but clothes, furniture, used toys, or whatever, depends on the generosity of others. Giving—rather than throwing away—acquisitions so that they can be incorporated into new systems of value is generally a product of personal patterns of consumption that are not simply excessive but also wasteful. The capacity to overconsume is a minority privilege that masks not only the conditions of production—who makes the things we·desire and in what conditions—but also the ecological consequences of an economy driven by the logic of growth at all costs. Recycling gives recognition to the voluntary gestures of the overconsuming householder, but it *forgets* the gifts of those who suffer to produce commodities and the natural resources that are exploited to make them.

These factors would seem to be enough for us to abandon the idea of recycling as a gift. It appears to meet all of Diprose's criteria for a debased generosity. Recycling depends on selective forgetting; it does not contest the social and environmental inequities that support overconsumption. Its ethico-political effects perpetuate an asymmetrical distribution of recognition, resources, and power. Analyzing recycling in terms of a gift economy confirms Luke's pessimistic assessment.

Despite this assessment, there are other ways in which the concept of generosity can be framed. Diprose argues that a *corporeal* approach to generosity challenges the aporia of the gift. This approach not only escapes the limits of the social contract, it also foregrounds social justice questions in a more radical and productive way. Corporeal generosity "is not reducible to an economy of exchange between sovereign individuals. Rather, it is an openness to others that not only precedes and establishes communal relations but constitutes the self as open to otherness."[35]

Three elements shape Diprose's corporeal generosity. First, generosity is a force for transformation only if it goes unrecognized. This means that it is not driven by deliberate choice or conscious intention. Rather, the openness to others that characterizes corporeal generosity is carnal and affective. Second, the asymmetrical relations of recognition and forgetting that underpin giving are a product of asymmetrical evaluations of different bodies—and, I would add, of asymmetrical evaluations of human as opposed to nonhuman resources. In excessive consumption the exploitation of human *and* natural resources is forgotten. Finally, this network of social discrimination and inequity operates in and through the normalization of bodies. Challenging this injustice depends on intercorporeal relations that are open to difference, that are affective, and that overcome self-sovereignty and the egoism that underpins it.

Is it possible, then, to develop an ethics of waste predicated on corporeal generosity? If we accept that the existing waste habit of recycling cannot escape the logic of obligation and reciprocity, what transformations are necessary to challenge the symbolic capital that recycling generates? How might the righteousness of recyclers be undone? Does the habit of recycling contain possibilities for more radical and just waste practices in which a corporeal generosity might emerge?

Recycling is an example of a minor change in habits around waste. Its implementation involved a different bodily disposition and performance, a different way of doing things with old paper and empty containers. In previous sections the meanings of this practice, the different kinds of calculative agency and socio-technical relations that it produced, are examined. On the basis of this analysis it is wrong to assume that agency comes before actions, that the thinking self makes the body change its habits. As Diprose says: "The self does not have an identity except through action. The deed, act or performance is the self actualized."[36] Despite all the representations of recycling as a new waste policy smoothly transmitted to the population, my argument is that it was through changes in the bodily actions and habits of waste management that the recycler was constituted. The performance of a new identity emerged through acts and an assemblage of different material and technical relations. And while these acts have come to be framed within the logic of a social contract and the calculation of virtue, within them another, more corporeal, form of generosity might lurk.

Diprose's criteria for a corporeal generosity offer an inspiring framework for how a more just and sustainable ethics of waste could function. Rather than a minor change in habits that confers virtue on the dutiful recycler, waste practices based on corporeal generosity would involve a body that was open to the difference of waste and the nonhuman world; a body that was aware of how its ways of living depended on the gifts of others. It would mean a body that was not indifferent to waste's alterity but aware, instead, of the intersubjective links that always connect us to what we discard.

In making us handle waste differently recycling *has* made us open to the materiality of waste in ways that chucking it in the bin denies. The boundary between self and waste becomes ambiguous when new habits allow wasted things to become more familiar, to imprint us with their phenomenological specificity: the cardboard box that's surprisingly tough to crush, the sharp edge of the empty can, the dress that is being given to charity that still feels and smells new. In the physical work of recycling, waste things become incorporated into new movements and habits as the body becomes open to waste. This doesn't necessarily make us think about how most of the waste we make comes from exploited labor and goes to an exploited nature. But it does entangle us in new relations and bodily practices that could be the first small step toward a more radical ethics of waste that is based on corporeal generosity rather than just "doing the right thing."

NOTES

1. Mary Douglas, *Purity and Danger* (London: Routledge and Kegan Paul, 1966), 2.

2. Of course this idea of fixed structuralist oppositions is a fantasy; the minute the rubbish is gone it starts building up again, it reappears. Or you find the bin is only

three-quarters empty, or bits of rubbish missed the truck and are strewn on the road. The boundary between clean and dirty is not at all stable.

3. Steven Connor, *Theory and Cultural Value* (Oxford: Basil Blackwell, 1992), 57.

4. John Law, "Economics as Interference," in *Cultural Economy*, ed. Paul du Gay and Michael Pryke (London: Sage, 2002).

5. Law, "Economics as Interference," 25.

6. Susan Strasser, *Waste and Want: A Social History of Trash* (New York: Metropolitan Books, 1999), 21.

7. Strasser, *Waste and Want*, 57.

8. Strasser, *Waste and Want*, 74.

9. Strasser, *Waste and Want*, 109.

10. Devleena Ghosh and Stephen Muecke, "Natural Logics of the Indian Ocean" (unpublished paper presented at the Environments and Ecologies Symposium, Adelaide, Australia, 2004).

11. Vance Packard, *The Waste Makers* (Middlesex: Penguin, 1963).

12. See Strasser's useful reading of this book in *Waste and Want*, 274–78.

13. Packard, *The Waste Makers*, 20.

14. Packard, *The Waste Makers*, 236.

15. Australian Government, *Report on the Implementation of a National Kerbside Recycling Strategy* (Canberra, Australia: National Kerbside Recycling Taskforce, 1982), 7.

16. See chapter 2 for an analysis of how recycling involved the formation of a new conscience around waste.

17. John Tierney, "Recycling Is Garbage," *New York Times Magazine*, June 30, 1996.

18. Tierney, "Recycling Is Garbage," 24–29.

19. *Waste Paper in Australia* (Sydney: Ausnewz Pulp and Paper, 1998), 161.

20. Barbara Herrnstein Smith, *Contingencies of Value* (Cambridge, MA: Harvard University Press, 1988), 133.

21. Smith, *Contingencies of Value*, 133.

22. Australian Government, *Interim Report on Paper Recycling* (Canberra: Australian Government Publishers, 1990), 43.

23. Law, "Economics as Interference," 24.

24. Sandra Buckley, "A Guided Tour of the Kitchen: Seven Japanese Domestic Tales," *Environment and Planning D: Society and Space* 14 (1996): 441–61.

25. Buckley, "Guided Tour," 448. Much of the empirical material for Buckley's paper comes from Eyal Ben-Ari, "A Bureaucrat in Every Japanese Kitchen," *Administration and Society* 21, no. 4 (1990): 472–92.

26. Buckley, "Guided Tour," 448.

27. Sandra Buckley, "Waste and Recycling," in *Encyclopedia of Contemporary Japanese Culture*, ed. Sandra Buckley (London: Routledge, 2002), 560.

28. Timothy Luke, "Green Consumerism: Ecology and the Ruse of Recycling," in *In the Nature of Things*, ed. Jane Bennett and William Chaloupka (Minneapolis: University of Minnesota Press, 1993), 170.

29. Andrew Ross, "The Lonely Hour of Scarcity," in *Real Love: In Pursuit of Cultural Justice* (London: Routledge, 1998), 167.

30. John Frow, "Invidious Distinction: Waste, Difference and Classy Stuff," in *Culture and Waste: The Creation and Destruction of Value*, ed. Gay Hawkins and Stephen Muecke (Lanham, MD: Rowman and Littlefield, 2002), 33.

31. Jacques Derrida, *Given Time* (Chicago: University of Chicago Press, 1992).

32. Rosalyn Diprose, *Corporeal Generosity* (New York: State University of New York Press, 2002).

33. Diprose, *Corporeal Generosity*, 2.

34. Diprose, *Corporeal Generosity*, 8.

35. Diprose, *Corporeal Generosity*, 4.

36. Diprose, *Corporeal Generosity*, 61.

6

Worms

In chapter 1, "An Overflowing Bin," I briefly outline Deleuze and Parnet's notion of politics as "active experimentation." Their philosophy privileges tactical practices and improvisation at the micropolitical level as important sources of change. This resonates with Foucault's insistence that it is always possible to experiment and go beyond the limits that are imposed on us. In doing this we are not claiming an essential freedom but taking up the possibility of new modes of self-direction and cultivation that express a "reflective heteronomy."[1] In subsequent chapters I explore examples of active experimentation with waste. The toilet festivals of Mumbai show how do-it-yourself sanitation transforms slum dwellers' relations to their waste and themselves. The minor practices of gleaning and making do reveal radically different person-thing relations. The care and attention involved in managing a compost pile turn disgust at decay into pleasure in renewal. These examples show how different techniques of waste management can disrupt destructive and ethically thoughtless practices. They reveal the possibilities of waste sensibilities that are not characterized by an ethos of disposability and denial.

Some of these techniques are driven by poverty and marginalization. I have no desire to underestimate the force of desperate necessity. Nor do I want to invite overconsuming waste makers to find authenticity or salvation in the conditions of the poor and marginal. Rather, I want to think about how different modes of living with waste engage the energy of experimentation and reveal its impacts on bodies and ethics. My aim in this chapter is to examine the politics of active experimentation in more depth in order to consider what a more sustainable and just ethics of waste looks and feels like. How does it contest the ethos of disposability and denial? How does it reveal a different relation to change and transience? How does such a politics manage the relation between waste and loss in ways that affirm life? How does it inaugurate different relations to the material everyday?

The tools I have used to do political analysis throughout this book have had little to do with repressive and totalizing conceptions of power. While there is no doubt that the logic of commodity culture is fundamental to the massive amounts of waste produced every day and its destructive impacts, deterministic accounts of politics haven't been my focus. Rather, I've been concerned with what Connolly calls the "molecular movements of micropolitics," or the ways in which bodily affects and habits of self-cultivation shape ethical sensibilities and our relations with things and the world.[2] For Connolly, micropolitics occur at the level of detail, desire, feeling, and perception; and, he argues, this level is coextensive with wider macropolitical cultures. Macro- and micropolitics do not exist in a relation of opposition, nor should they be ranked on a scale of importance. They are interconnected, and "politics becomes most intensive and most fateful at those junctures where micropolitics and macropolitics intersect."[3]

Micropolitics emerge in the relational arts of the self, and these arts are always open to the possibility of change. They may not change in big, dramatic, revolutionary ways, but they change. They shift and move because they involve the dynamics of relations and the ongoing work of crafting a self. A recognition of the self as a product of relations and interdependency is not, however, guaranteed. Many of the minor practices we engage in day after day contribute to stabilizing the self, affirming identity through the repetitive reassurance of habits. The relation that is enacted in these habits often involves an arrogant assertion of a sovereign self separated from the world. This "transcendental egoism," as Connolly calls it, blinds us to our dependence on otherness, making it difficult to see how much our identity emerges in and through relations of differentiation. Diprose describes this relation of fundamental dependence in this way: "As one's identity and social value are produced through a differentiation between the self and the other then the identity of the self is dispersed into the other."[4] In other examples explored in previous chapters I trace how various waste practices blind us to our dependence on the otherness of waste and our fundamental interconnections with it. The effect of these practices is to deny relationality and interconnection, leading to a cavalier disavowal of the impacts of our waste habits.

How then to nurture a micropolitics of the self that is aware of our fundamental interconnections with waste and concerned to manage these connections in careful and sustainable ways? What kinds of tactics and active experimentation would be needed to open up the self to waste, to contest arrogant egoism and the exploitation and destruction it breeds? As I've argued, a first step is to notice waste, to let it capture our attention. For in that momentary glimpse, or shudder, or rush of feeling, a changed relation is enacted. Something flows across the membranes of supposed separation that Patton calls the "connective power of relationality."[5] He uses this term to explain Deleuze and Guattari's emphasis on the in-between or the indeterminate conjunction that subtends all relations: *and*.[6] For Deleuze and Guattari the in-between is where things happen, it is a field of emergence. However, recognizing this connection, feeling the relational dynamics in between yourself *and* waste, is not necessarily enough to transform that relation. It can often lead to a virulent and reactive assertion of separation and mastery. Something else must happen to nurture an ethos of positive engagement with waste, to trigger a relation of openness and care, and to encourage the cultivation of new habits.

Perhaps that something is recognition of the how the affective responses that waste can trigger disrupt oppositions between self and world or self and waste. When we notice waste, or when it touches the most visceral registers of being and unsettles us, we are reminded of the body's intensities and multiplicities. These affects can feel like a qualitative overspill, an excess that escapes the knowable, manageable subject. Recognizing the affective dimensions of waste makes trouble for all those epistemologies that begin with the knowing subject ready to act on the world, ready to "do the right thing"; for the affective body does not simply stand as subject to the world's objectivity, it is an "articulated body in transition." This is Brian Massumi's term, and he goes on to explain how affect *is* relationality, how to be in the world is to be in an ever-unfolding relation. Affect, then, can disrupt oppositions as it opens us up to the processual rhythms of being. It can allow us to see how we are *in* and *of* the world.[7]

Sensing how we are in and of the world, not separate and the center of it, means sensing our similarities and interdependence with waste. It means sensing the inevitability of our own wasting. Wasted things in all their various stages of decay—rotting, broken, abandoned—speak of time and endings. I've argued that to be blind to waste and its materiality is to be blind to death and the fact of loss. The refusal to notice waste is also the refusal to notice the finality of life. In this way, waste defines the scope of ethics. Waste is *inevitable*, and how we deal with this, what sort of calculations and values we create to make this incontrovertible fact meaningful, is the terrain of ethics. While religion and other grand moral narratives redeem waste and loss with righteous declarations, this is not ethics. Redemption does not necessarily help us live with loss. Its idealism can overprotect us; stop us from accepting the world as it is, stop us from acknowledging the ways in which death is not salvation but part of life. Ethics, rather than traditional moralities, tend to be more modest, more creative, and more relational. This makes them more available to a realistic acknowledgment of finitude, because it's through ethical experimentation in ways of living that it becomes possible to develop an affirmative acceptance of loss, a simple recognition of the contingency of life and the paradoxical interconnections between destruction and renewal. David Halperin has an incisive account of this distinction between ethics and morality in relation to waste:

> The difference between ethics and morality lies in their differing attitudes to value and to waste. According to a moralistic perspective, life is not wasted if it is lived in the service of value. Value gives transcendental meaning to life and redeems the loss of it. An ethical perspective, by contrast, is one that measures, assesses and adjudicates among the diverse concrete practices of living one's life, the various calculations used to determine how exactly to throw it away.[8]

What, then, does an ethics of waste that accepts loss look like? If living is shadowed by the reality of death, how might death and loss be acknowledged, and how might this contribute to a positive rather than a destructive ethic of waste? In this chapter I want to explore some examples of waste management that contest the dominant ethos of disposal, distance, and denial. These examples reflect not only active experimentation but also a different relational dynamic between the self and waste, a concern to manage waste in ways that are attentive to what Adam Phillips calls "the arts of transience."[9]

THE ARTS OF TRANSIENCE

Before I get to these examples I want to outline what Phillips means by the arts of transience. The development of this concept in his book *Darwin's Worms* is stimulating and inspiring. He shows how it is possible to pursue the connections between waste and loss without recourse to despair or moralism. Phillips's account of how Darwin and Freud thought about change and transience shows how ethics infuse the most ordinary practices. His emphasis on the "arts" of transience resonates with Foucault's account of ethics as the arts of living. It reminds us that a key element of a sustainable ethic of waste is facilitating careful transition in the most ordinary gestures of daily life. Phillips shows how, in giving up the delusions of immortality and purity (which are doomed to continuous failure), we are compelled to invent ways of living that presume interdependency, intermingling, and loss. And scenes of loss—big and small—provide powerful opportunities for such invention. As he says, "Losing is an art, it inspires a new quality of attention."[10]

Transience is everywhere; things change. We can see it in our bodies; we can see it in the broken remains of objects that once were new. Phillips's question is: Why is this so daunting? What is our relationship to change; how could we become more at ease with endings? Using the work of Darwin and Freud he explores how these two key thinkers of secular modernism tried to figure out the place of death in the ways we live. Rejecting the comfort of religious redemption and nostalgia for an idealized pastoral nature, both sought to explain how it was possible to retain interest and happiness in the world once you acknowledged death and suffering. If you accept that death is one of the organizing principles of life, how do you escape the pull of grief or nihilism? Phillips suggests that we can do so by becoming realistic, by accepting transience rather than transcendence, by learning to live with death in ways that affirm life.

The most powerful evocation of this thesis is in Phillips's reading of Darwin's book *Formation of Vegetable Mould through the Action of Worms, with Observations on Their Habits* (1881).[11] In Darwin's theories of earthworms, Phillips finds an account of an exemplary moral universe. He argues that Darwin's exploration of the biological functions of worms is also, implicitly, a moral and philosophical analysis of the meanings of transition. Rather than dismiss worms as trivial because they occupy the bottom of hierarchies—high-low, surface-underground—Darwin rejects these binaries and argues that worms are sophisticated and heroic laborers that manage transition, or the space *in between* these opposed terms. He refuses the typical association of worms with lowliness, death, and decay and sees them, instead, as fundamental to the making and remaking of the world. Their constant digesting work reveals another sort of loss, a loss that is not destructive but transformative, loss that is also renewal. In praising the inexhaustible work that makes the earth fertile Darwin celebrates the resilience and inventiveness of nature. He replaces a Christian creation myth with a secular maintenance myth: worms create the earth, not God. What Darwin finds in worms, according to Phillips, is a moral universe predicated on *collaborative generosity*. Worms' digestion is not a form of altruism, it is gratuitously virtuous; they provide good things without intending to and show us the paradoxical interconnections between destruction and renewal. Despite their thoroughgoing involvement with decay, worms are on the side of life: "They buried to renew: they digested to restore."[12]

WORM STORIES

I want to tell some worm stories now that show the arts of transience in action. My aim is to think about their ethical significance, to reflect on how they alter ways of living and embodiment. How have worms been deployed in a politics of active experimentation with waste?

In a very old house in Sydney a few miles from the city center sits the now famous sustainable house. It's a typical nineteenth-century terrace from the outside, narrow and unremarkable. Inside it looks pretty similar to most old houses occupied by a busy family. It's been stylishly renovated with all mod cons, the glass sliding doors at the rear looking onto a lovely landscaped bush garden. But beneath all this inner urban normality is a vastly different infrastructure making the house function: providing power and water and dealing with waste. The house runs on solar power collected from roof panels, with any excess going back into the grid. Potable water is collected from the roof and filtered using sophisticated carbon technology. All waste water from the house flows into a Dowmus waste system, which uses earthworms and microorganisms to break down and filter human effluent, gray water, and food scraps. This waste management system sits outside the back door. It looks like a long garden seat (and that is another function) running along the length of the tiny backyard. Inside worms manage the household waste. At the end of the system, water, which is mostly free of pathogens, is pumped through a compact ultraviolet light disinfector to ensure that it is completely sterile. This water is then used to wash clothes and flush the toilet, with any excess pumped into a reed bed at the bottom of the garden.

While this house is exemplary and pretty unusual in a very dense urban area, it is not exceptional as far as examples of sustainability go. It does all the right things—uses renewable energy, collects rainwater rather than letting it run away down a storm-water system, and manages its waste on-site. This house sits very lightly on the ground; it shows us how we can live far more sustainably without sacrificing "quality of life." It still has a bidet and a dishwasher; being inside it doesn't feel like participating in an alternative lifestyle. Assessments of the house have calculated that it saves over 26,500 gallons of water from Sydney's water supply, keeps more than 21,000 gallons of storm water out of Sydney Harbour, and prevents more than 16,000 gallons of sewage from being pumped into the Pacific Ocean. If environmental ethics are about calculating the impacts of human practices on natural systems, then these figures are impressive.[13] There is no question that the residents of this house should have an easier conscience, but what about the impacts of these different systems on their habits? What does it mean to live with worms eating your shit outside your back door? How does the fact of a different technique for waste management reverberate across the bodies that live there?

When I first visited this house I went on one of its regular public tours. We were shown through the interior and invited to inspect the various systems keeping the house functioning. Then we went into the backyard, and someone asked about waste and whether the house was hooked up to the sewer. The owner showed us the six-foot-long worm farm masquerading as a garden seat. He lifted the lid and let us smell the fecund odor of decay. He poked around and showed us the worms heroically laboring. He collected some water from the end of the system and showed us how clean it was. "You could drink this," he declared. Everyone in the tour shuddered and then laughed with horror. Purity and danger were evoked, the excess of laughter releasing the tension of a taboo transgressed.

Here was a house where it was possible to see the arts of transience in action. Traditional systems of elimination that remove waste fast and invisibly were not in place. There were still underground drains, but they ended up in the backyard. Bodily waste in its most immediate and hazardous form remained hidden, but once it was subject to transformation into compost it was *present*; the worm farm occupied a significant space in the backyard. It was enclosed in an attractive box, it didn't smell, but its reality could not be denied. This household couldn't help but acknowledge waste, not in its brute physicality but as a fact of their daily lives, as something that required attention. You couldn't sustain an ethos of distance and denial in this house because its structural organization presumes a careful and ethical coexistence with waste.

All the quotidian rituals of caring for the worm farm, keeping it functioning efficiently, have impacts on bodies. They require new habits, different corporeal disciplines, and these reverberate across other registers of the self. It is hard for bodily waste to sustain the same level of symbolic force as abject horrifying matter when its management, once it leaves your body, remains your responsibility. Instead, one has to become realistic about it, give it a certain quality of attention. The dynamics of repression are diminished in this new relation with bodily waste. As I've argued elsewhere, different technologies of waste management show how habits and symbolic systems intersect and how these points of intersection can transform affects and micropolitics.[14] Here was a family that had experimented with a different way of living with their waste. This didn't involve messiness or unboundedness, the collapse of all boundaries, or the collapse of a notion of waste. Rather, it involved different technical systems, bodily performances, calculations of value, and the relations between these. Waste in this house wasn't disgusting or abhorrent. It was in transition, in between contaminating and productive. And facilitating that transition involved two crucial things: lots and lots of worms and simple attentiveness. Through these two things a sustainable ethics of waste emerged.

Changes in one house or even hundreds won't save the planet. This is a common criticism of the sustainable house and other strategies that focus on individuals or families taking a stand and radically changing their daily practices. In fact, these strategies have sometimes been interpreted as the privatization of public problems. This is not my position. I would challenge it by arguing that the adoption of strategies at the micropolitical level of the home and the body reverberates across larger political culture in a multiplicity of ways. When the sustainable house is featured on a national lifestyle show, when people who have been on a tour of it talk to friends, when Internet sites showcase it, it impacts on new constituencies. Micropolitics shape an inter-subjective ethos of politics. This intersubjective ethos occurs in conversations, in the media, in myriad relations in which practical examples of different ways of managing waste undermine normalized and exploitative practices and nur-ture receptivity to change.

But what about structural solutions? What about sustainable human waste management on a large scale? In Granville Township in Pennsylvania the Sewer and Water Department decided in 2004 to solve its serious biowaste problem by signing a contract for a full-scale vermicomposting system, the first to be constructed in the United States. The existing sewer system used an aerobic sludge digestion facility that involved intermittent discharge into a river and the transfer of dewatered biosolids, or what was left over, to a land-fill. This landfill was rapidly reaching capacity, and so an alternative solution to the problem of biosolid waste was required. Four vermiculture beds six feet wide and ninety-five feet long housing one thousand pounds of worms per bed were the solution.[15] This large-scale use of worms to manage a town's biosolids does not have any impact on householders; it makes no claims on them, and it won't change their habits. But it does show an important shift at the macropolitical level of local systems of governmentality. It shows a will-ingness to embrace a more sustainable technology, and whether this was done for cost-saving reasons or environmental concerns is irrelevant. The fact is that worms are being productively used to facilitate the arts of transience on a mass scale where once dumping was the solution.

The images used to promote the Granville project show the giant worm farms housed in a shed. There is lots of engineering in evidence: conveyer belts to move and spread the mix, trays and another conveyer system to col-lect the castings, which are then stabilized and sold as agricultural fertilizer. This is a potent example of how nature is always differentially mixed into cul-ture. All this technology doesn't diminish the great significance of the work being done by those worms as they facilitate transition. In those giant indus-trial worm farms heightened life and heightened death *go together*; the pro-found interconnections between destruction and renewal are everywhere evident. Perhaps this system exemplifies what Phillips calls "the ordinary sub-lime." He uses this term to explain the difficulties Darwin had accounting for experiences of things that overwhelm and overawe us once God drops out of the picture.

It is the immediate (in the literal sense) participation of nature in the experience of men and women that Darwin is promoting. But it is the ordinary sublime of transience that he singles out; there is nothing more ordinary, more natural, than that we should have experiences that no one, not even God, understands: experiences that satisfy us because they overwhelm us, experiences we value because they are strange.[16]

The ordinary sublime of transience is what worms show us. To witness worms at work, whether on a big or small scale, is to encounter the philosophical resonance of biological processes. Worms are the penultimate loss managers, and they give us a powerful example of how quotidian and inevitable change is. And in this very ordinariness we can see how loss and change can be experienced without denial or disgust or despair, and without recourse to grand moral rhetoric. We can see how waste can contribute to renewal, how it can be generative.

I've argued that current waste habits protect us from encountering change. Their predictability and comfort is predicated on technologies of streamlined removal that allow us to avoid the transition that wasted things will inevitably undergo. Most acts of disposal involve relations with technology or containers, not the waste itself. We experience elimination and removal but not decay and change. Managing a worm farm disrupts this. When you live with worms you enter into a different means of engagement with waste: your bodily and kitchen by-products become their food, their waste becomes your garden fertilizer. You have to live with your waste a little more carefully so as to facilitate its effective transition by worms, and in these habits a calmer acceptance of your own transience might be nurtured.

LIVING WITH DESTRUCTION

Worms are good for seeing the links between philosophy and biology. They make a politics of active experimentation easy. It's simple to nurture the generative possibilities of waste when you can harness the generosity of worms; they encourage an ethic of sustainability by default. But worms don't eat broken fridges, or outmoded computers or mountains of plastic drink bottles. Being on the side of life means that they facilitate transition as a form of productive return. They are no help in confronting the destructive reality of waste on a mass scale, whereby dumped dead objects sink into an endless afterlife. Worms cannot deal with the ecological consequences of commodity cultures—the accumulation of wasted things and the toxicity and ruins such cultures create. The exploitation of human and environmental resources in the name of "progress" reveals a will to destruction that defiles *both* life and death.[17] The will to destruction inhibits the generative possibilities of death and loss that worms exemplify with such force.

In shifting now to an analysis of waste as destructive, my aim is not to find examples of active experimentation but to understand how commodity relations actually inhibit the development of these minor practices. The logics of commodity cultures make the arts of transience difficult to enact in relation to nonputrescible waste. This is because the short life of the commodity defines transience *not* as renewal but as endless disappearance and replacement. And it is this slight but significant distinction that signals how commodity cultures produce particular experiences of time, loss, and the past. An ethos of consumption teaches us how to make a fetish of the new, how to live with constant change, and how to adapt to the temporality of serial replacement and disposability. When the ever new is ever the same, transience is experienced not as cyclical repetition in the interest of regeneration but as "extreme temporal attenuation."[18] And it is this phenomenological experience of consumption as turnover and repetition that blinds us to the will to destruction that underwrites it.

Walter Benjamin offers one of the most important analyses of transience and destruction in commodity cultures. In several key texts he speculates on how the rise of commodity culture has displaced nature's transitoriness onto commodities. Susan Buck-Morss reads this work with insight.[19] Her account of Benjamin's thinking on fashion traces how he sees the reified commodity as a kind of reversal of biology; the living human potential for change becomes alienated and appears instead as a quality of inorganic objects. The cult of the new and the worship of youth are fundamental to the modern commodity, and one effect of this is the *denial* of organic change. As Benjamin says of modernity: "This time doesn't want to know death. . . . Fashion mocks death."[20] In commodity cultures the creativity and transiency of nature, which are a source of life, become seriality and the cult of the new, which deny the fact of death at the same time as they fuel destruction.

Benjamin is fascinated with the other side of commodification: the mortification of matter that is no longer fashionable. He sees in rubbish the death mask of the commodity, and he shows how these abandoned everyday things could be used to think with. Unlike so many contemporary theorists of material culture Benjamin takes the debris of mass culture seriously. He sees it as a source of both concrete historical referents and philosophical insight.[21] He is interested in how to figure the destructiveness of commodity culture, not so much in terms of economic exploitation, but in terms of how the magical value and fetish value of commodities are experienced and extinguished. Like Phillips, Benjamin makes a case for destruction as a condition of possibility for the experience of life and philosophical truth. He is interested in the creative potential of change, the ways in which destruction can produce new relations to things and new insights. The destruction of the aura of the artwork through mechanical reproduction, for example, opened up the possibility of changed relations with the image and the chance to perceive ordinary things in radically new ways.[22]

But the rise of modernity and commodity culture was also catastrophic. The destruction of cities in the name of modernization obliterated the past and revealed the fragility of things that seemed permanent. The industrial system alienated people from the realities of production and turned things into reified objects of desire. The rise of the fashion system and the novelty of the new accelerated obsolescence shortened the life of things. Modernity's "progress" was continual change as eternal recurrence. Buck-Morss describes Benjamin's thoughts on catastrophe in the *Passagen-Werk* like this: "Transiency *without* progress, a relentless pursuit of 'novelty' that brings nothing new in history— in making visible the outlines of *this* temporality, Benjamin provides the direct counterimage to an approaching heaven-on-earth."[23]

If consumer culture was not heaven on earth as promised, if it trapped people in the "deadly repetitiveness of time," or a perpetual now, how could its catastrophic effects be challenged?[24] What kinds of political practice might overcome this? How might a concept of the new as radical dislocation disrupt the relentless continuity of transiency without progress? In pursuing these questions Benjamin draws on diverse sources from Marxist historiography to surrealism. I cannot do justice to his thinking on the nature of politics and historical experience here.[25] My concern is with what he thought about the specific role of commodities in recasting social order. And in addressing this question wasted and decaying things, the detritus and debris of commodity culture, are of singular importance.

Benjamin's explanations of how commodities might confront and challenge us range from the apocalyptic to the everyday. His famous image of the Angel of History facing the past as wreckage, "while the pile of debris before him grows skyward," has been extensively analyzed.[26] It prefigures not just a radical philosophy of history but, also, as Paul Magee suggests, an environmentalist discourse on waste: "The Angel shows such a subject his or her *barbarism* in the 'pile of debris' that is the present continuous tense of the everyday."[27]

But the small examples are more suggestive for thinking about the changes that might happen when subjects encounter discarded things. Benjamin's thoughts on surrealist bricolage in "Dream Kitsch" trace the energy surrealism was able to invest in everyday debris. And he shows how these avant-garde practices disrupted perception and gave ordinary things a compelling power over humans.[28] His account of avant-garde practices concurs with Connolly's definition of micropolitics. Benjamin is aware of the political possibilities of small changes in perception and experience, of what might happen when familiar things are seen differently. He recognizes the political possibilities of shock and wonder, the ways in which these affects can be the source of minor transformations.

In his essay on surrealism he examines how confrontations with wasted things can crystallize the dynamics of commodity value. Bill Brown summarizes the key argument of this essay like this: "Benjamin recognised that the gap between the function of objects and the desires congealed there became clear *only when those objects became outmoded*."[29] Wasted things can make us suddenly aware of the vagaries of desire; they can let us see the material substance out of which commodities emerge. But is this enough to change the destructive logic of commodification, to make us aware of the impacts of disposability as transience without renewal? Who can say? All that can be argued is that these moments engage us in different relations with commodities that could be a source of more self-conscious material practices.

Benjamin wants a new materialism, and he sees evidence of it at work in how children play with wasted things. He interprets these games and inventions not in psychological terms but as political and historical examples of how another materiality could be created. Again I am drawn to Brown's analysis because it captures so beautifully Benjamin's hope in imagining a different way of living with things:

One must imagine that within the child's "tactile tryst" the substantiality of things emerges for the first time, and that this is the condition for reshaping the material world we inhabit. One must imagine that this *experience* in the everyday foretells a different human *existence*. If the use value of an object amounts to its preconceived utility, then its misuse value should be understood as the unforeseeable potential within the object, part of an uncompleted dream.[30]

Children's play with waste and other things is an example of active experimentation because it involves a process of creating new meanings and relations. It parallels the practices of gleaning and making do that I explore in chapter 4. All these activities show how waste can provoke new uses and engagements. In play and *misuse value*, as Brown calls it, another materiality is created. Benjamin reads this as politically salient; in the child's world he sees the radical possibilities of different ways of being with things. This different way of being involves a more immediate appreciation of the qualitative and substantial reality of the thing. It is less mediated and reified; it is about use value, not exchange value. And this is its implicit challenge to commodity relations and the alienation and abstraction that they generate.

There is, however, a danger in this opposition between direct appreciation of material things and alienated consumption of commodities. It can too easily fuel a disenchantment narrative about commodity relations as essentially bad. While I completely accept environmentalism's critiques of the destructive impacts of commodification, one of my aims in this book is to think about the other effects and possibilities of commodity relations. I have taken my lead from Jane Bennett, whose phenomenology of consumption emphasizes the ambiguities of commodity relations, the unpredictable and disturbing effects they can generate, and the political experiments they might provoke.[31]

Like Benjamin, Bennett does not dismiss commodities' capacity to enchant as mere manipulation. Their fetish and magical qualities might be *precisely* where new affects and relations could surface. Benjamin sees the wasted fragments and debris of modern urban life as one site where the contingency and fragility of commodity value is exposed. Bennett sees advertisements as a site where the animation of things can remind us of the liveliness of matter. Both these thinkers accept and explore with insight the deadening and destructive effects of consumption. Commodity cultures create ruins at the same time as they make us blind to this. But, Benjamin and Bennett argue, commodities can also engage us with their material and magical qualities; offer us pleasure and real sensual delights. These experiences remind us of how commodities make claims on us beyond the immediacy of desire and purchase. In fitting them into our lives we have to figure out how to possess them in more than economic terms. The attachments and affects we create in our everyday habits with things challenge accounts of consumers as dulled and stupefied; they reveal a complexity in material relations that cannot be reduced to the cultural logic of capitalism.

And this complexity surfaces in the experiences we can have of objects that somehow challenge the ethos of disposability and denial. The very act of attention, of noticing what we so often don't see, captures us in different relations with objects that can become new networks of obligation. This book explores some of the affects and calculations that can emerge in these networks and energize a different ethics of waste. Feeling moved by a dancing plastic bag, feeling disgusted by an ocean streaked with human waste, feeling surprised by the wondrous beauty of a dumped potato, feeling good about recycling—these various affects and responses reverberate through the body, disrupting careless habits and inviting us to reflect on how our selfhood is caught up with waste.

Over the last thirty years waste has been problematized. These various problematizations have informed governmental programs on waste reduction and householder education. They have led to a range of moral codes about how we should be around our waste. These codes have been enfolded with new domestic habits and new circuits of guilt and conscience about waste. The changes in behavior that have resulted from these new codes and disciplines have led to different waste management practices that have no doubt made a difference. But moral codes are pretty crude instruments for change, they can breed resentment and they can involve unthinking obedience to rules. They can also identify very restricted sources as the motivation for moral actions. In the case of waste this has most often been nature in crisis. However, in the appeal to save the earth, to make a gesture to the planet, our complex interconnections with waste are often denied or displaced.

This book has explored what happens when *waste* rather than nature is the motivation for new actions. This has led to a focus on ethics as relations of self-cultivation rather than on morality as categorical imperatives. It has also led to an investigation of how we live with waste; its place in techniques of the self; how it is implicated in embodiment, habits, and the material everyday;

and how it can unsettle our confidence and mastery. In many of the situations surveyed here waste isn't a phobic object. It's part of a relation in which we sense our interdependence with what we discard and feel the force of time and transience. The singularity of these encounters, or "waste relations," makes prescriptive definitions of a "proper" ethics of waste impossible. There are many different ways in which the ethos of disposability, distance, and denial can be challenged, many different ways in which our waste micropractices could be transformed. But for this to happen, for a less destructive ethics of waste to emerge, awareness of the arts of transience is crucial. Whatever form this takes, cultivating a careful and generous attention to loss is a good way to start.

NOTES

1. This is Jane Bennett's term. She uses it in her excellent discussion of ethics and micropractices in chapter 7 of *The Enchantment of Modern Life* (Princeton, NJ: Princeton University Press, 2001), 146.

2. William Connolly, *Why I Am Not a Secularist* (Minneapolis: University of Minnesota Press, 1999), 149.

3. Connolly, *Why*, 149.

4. Rosalyn Diprose, *Corporeal Generosity* (Albany: State University of New York Press, 2002).

5. Paul Patton, *Deleuze and the Political* (London: Routledge, 2000), 10.

6. Patton, *Deleuze*, 10.

7. Brian Massumi, "Too Blue: Colour Patch for an Expanded Empiricism," *Cultural Studies* 14, no. 2 (2000): 177–226.

8. David Halperin, "Out of Australia," in *Culture and Waste*, eds. Gay Hawkins and Stephen Meucke (Lanham, MD: Rowman and Littlefield, 2002), 6.

9. Adam Phillips, *Darwin's Worms* (London: Faber and Faber, 1999).

10. Phillips, *Darwin's Worms*, 120.

11. Charles Darwin, *Formation of Vegetable Mould through the Action of Worms, with Observations on Their Habits* (1881; reprint, Chicago: Chicago University Press, 1985).

12. Phillips, *Darwin's Worms*, 56.

13. Michael Linke, "Sydney's Sustainable House," *ReNew*, July–September 1997, 14–17.

14. Gay Hawkins, "Down the Drain: Shit and the Politics of Disturbance," in Hawkins and Meucke, *Culture and Waste*, 51.

15. Larry E. Craig, "Granville Township's Vermicomposting System," *Central Pennsylvania Water Quality Association Newsletter* 16, no. 3 (July 2004).

16. Phillips, *Darwin's Worms*, 24.

17. Deborah Bird Rose, "What If the Angel of History Were a Dog?" (unpublished paper presented at Environments and Ecologies Symposium, Adelaide, Australia, July 3–4, 2004), 3.

18. Susan Buck-Morss, *The Dialectics of Seeing* (Cambridge, MA: MIT Press, 1991), 65.

19. Buck-Morss, *Dialectics of Seeing*, 98.

20. Walter Benjamin, "Passagen-Werk," quoted in Buck-Morss, *Dialectics of Seeing*, 99.

21. Buck-Morss, *Dialectics of Seeing*, 4–5.

22. Walter Benjamin, "The Work of Art in the Age of Mechanical Reproduction," in *Illuminations*, trans. Harry Zohn (London: Fontana, 1977).

23. Buck-Morss, *Dialectics of Seeing*, 96 (emphasis in the original).

24. Buck-Morss, *Dialectics of Seeing*, 96.

25. For an excellent account of Benjamin's thinking on the political implications of modernity's temporality of the now see Peter Osborne, "Small-scale Victories, Large-scale Defeats," in *Destruction and Experience*, ed. Andrew Benjamin and Perter Osborne (Manchester: Clinamen, 2000).

26. Walter Benjamin, *Illuminations*, 259.

27. Paul Magee, *From Here to Tierra Del Fuego* (Urbana: University of Illinois Press, 2000), 34.

28. Walter Benjamin, "Dream Kitsch," in *Selected Writings*, ed. Michael Jennings and Gary Smith (Cambridge, MA: MIT Press, 1999).

29. Bill Brown, "Thing Theory," *Critical Inquiry* 28 (Autumn 2001): 13 (my emphasis).

30. Bill Brown, "How to Do Things with Things (A Toy Story)," *Critical Inquiry* 25, (Summer 1998): 955–56 (emphasis in the original).

31. Bennett, *Enchantment*, chapter 6.

Bibliography

Appadurai, Arjun. "Deep Democracy." *Public Culture* 14, no. 1 (Winter 2002).

"Are You a Good Sort?" Leaflet. New South Wales Waste Service, n.d.

Australian Government. *Interim Report on Paper Recycling.* Canberra: Australian Government Publishers, 1990.

———. *Report on the Implementation of a National Kerbside Recycling Strategy.* Canberra: Australian Government Publishers, 1982.

Beder, Sharon. *Toxic Fish and Sewer Surfing.* Sydney: Allen and Unwin, 1989.

Ben-Ari, Eyal. "A Bureaucrat in Every Japanese Kitchen." *Administration and Society* 21, no. 4 (1990): 472–92.

Benjamin, Walter. "Dream Kitsch." In *Selected Writings,* edited by Michael Jennings and Gary Smith. Cambridge, MA: MIT Press, 1999.

———. "The Work of Art in the Age of Mechanical Reproduction." In *Illuminations,* translated by Harry Zohn. London: Fontana, 1977.

Bennett, Jane. *The Enchantment of Modern Life.* Princeton, NJ: Princeton University Press, 2001.

———. "How Is It, Then, That We Still Remain Barbarians?" *Political Theory* 24, no. 4 (1996).

Bennett, Jane, and William Chaloupka, eds. *In The Nature of Things.* Minneapolis: University of Minnesota Press, 1993.

Bird Rose, Deborah. "Decolonizing the Discourse of Environmental Knowledge in Settler Societies." In Hawkins and Muecke, *Culture and Waste*.

———. "What If the Angel of History Were a Dog?" Unpublished paper presented at Environments and Ecologies in an Expanded Field Conference, Adelaide, Australia, July 3–4, 2004.

Bourdieu, Pierre. *The Logic of Practice*. Stanford, CA: Stanford University Press, 1990.

Brown, Bill. "How to Do Things with Things (A Toy Story)." *Critical Inquiry* 25 (Summer 1998): 935–64.

———. *A Sense of Things*. Chicago: University of Chicago Press, 2003.

———. "Thing Theory." *Critical Inquiry* 28 (Autumn 2001): 1–22.

Browne, Sheila. "Why POOO Raises a Stink." *Sydney Morning Herald*, February 15, 1990.

Buckley, Sandra. "A Guided Tour of the Kitchen: Seven Japanese Domestic Tales." *Environment and Planning D: Society and Space* 14 (1996): 441–61.

———. "Waste and Recycling." In *Encyclopedia of Contemporary Japanese Culture*, edited by Sandra Buckley. London: Routledge, 2002.

Buck-Morss, Susan. *The Dialectics of Seeing*. Cambridge, MA: MIT Press, 1991.

Butler, Judith. *The Psychic Life of Power*. California: Stanford University Press, 1997.

Calvino, Italo. "La Poubelle Agreee." In *The Road to San Giovanni*. London: Jonathon Cape, 1993.

Castree, Noel. "A Post-environmental Ethics?" *Ethics, Place and Environment* 6, no. 1 (March 2003).

Clarsen, Georgine. "Still Moving: Bush Mechanics in the Central Desert." *Australian Humanities Review*, March 2002, at www.lib.latrobe.edu.au/AHR/archive/Issue-March-2002/clarsen.html (accessed March 7, 2002).

Connolly, William. *Neuropolitics: Thinking, Culture, Speed*. Minneapolis: University of Minnesota Press, 2002.

———. *Why I Am Not a Secularist*. Minneapolis: University of Minnesota Press, 1999.

Connor, Steven. "Rough Magic: Bags." In *The Everyday Life Reader*, edited by Ben Highmore. London: Routledge, 2002.

———. *Theory and Cultural Value*. Oxford: Basil Blackwell, 1992.

Corbin, Alain. *The Foul and the Fragrant*. Cambridge, MA: Harvard University Press, 1986.

Craig, Larry E. "Granville Township's Vermicomposting System." *Central Pennsylvania Water Quality Association Newsletter* 16, no. 3 (July 2004).

Darke, Chris. "Refuseniks." *Sight and Sound* 11, no. 1 (January 2001): 30–31

Darwin, Charles. *Formation of Vegetable Mould through the Action of Worms, with Observations on Their Habits*. 1881. Reprint, Chicago: Chicago University Press, 1985.

Dean, Mitchell. "Foucault, Government and the Enfolding of Authority." In *Foucault and Political Reason*, edited by Andrew Barry, Thomas Osborne, and Nikolas Rose. Chicago: University of Chicago Press, 1996.

de Certeau, Michel. *The Practice of Everyday Life*. Berkeley: University of California Press, 1984.

Deleuze, Gilles. *Foucault*. Minneapolis: University of Minnesota Press, 1995.

Deleuze, Gilles, and Felix Guattari. *A Thousand Plateaus: Capitalism and Schizophrenia*. Translated by B. Massumi. London: Athlone, 1988.

Deleuze, Gilles, and Claire Parnet. *Dialogues 11*. Translated by Hugh Tomlinson and Barbara Habberjam. London: Continuum, 1987.

DeLillo, Don. *Underworld*. New York: Scribner, 1997.

Derrida, Jacques. *Given Time*. Chicago: University of Chicago Press, 1992.

Diprose, Rosalyn. *The Bodies of Women*. London: Routledge, 1994.

———. *Corporeal Generosity*. New York: State University of New York Press, 2002.

Douglas, Mary. *Purity and Danger*. London: Routledge and Kegan Paul, 1966.

du Gay, Paul, and Michael Pryke. *Cultural Economy*. London: Sage, 2002.

Foucault, Michel. *The Care of the Self*. Translated by Robert Hurley. New York: Vintage, 1988.

———. *The History of Sexuality*. Vol. 1, translated by Robert Hurley. New York: Penguin, 1981.

———. *The Use of Pleasure*. Translated by Robert Hurley. New York: Vintage, 1985.

Frow, John. "Invidious Distinction: Waste, Difference and Classy Stuff." In Hawkins and Muecke, *Culture and Waste.*

———. "A Pebble, a Camera, a Man Who Turns into a Telegraph Pole." *Critical Inquiry* 28 (Autumn 2001): 275.

Gatens, Moira. *Imaginary Bodies: Ethics, Power and Corporeality*. London: Routledge, 1996.

Ghosh, Devleena, and Stephen Muecke. "Natural Logics of the Indian Ocean." Unpublished paper presented at the Environments and Ecologies in an Expanded Field conference, Adelaide, Australia, July 3–4, 2004.

Gregson, Nicky, and Louise Crewe. *Second Hand Cultures*. Oxford: Berg, 2003.

Grosz, Elizabeth. *Architecture from the Outside*. Cambridge, MA: MIT Press, 2001.

Halperin, David. "Out of Australia." In Hawkins and Muecke, *Culture and Waste.*

Hawkins, Gay. "Down the Drain: Shit and the Politics of Disturbance." In Hawkins and Muecke, *Culture and Waste.*

———. "Plastic Bags: Living with Rubbish." *International Journal of Cultural Studies* 4, no. 1 (2001).

———. "Shit in Public." *Australian Humanities Review*. April 2004, at www.lib.latrobe .edu.au/AHR/archive/issue-April-2004/hawkins.html (accessed April 16, 2004).

Hawkins, Gay, and Stephen Muecke, eds. *Culture and Waste: The Creation and Destruction of Value*. Lanham MD: Rowman and Littlefield, 2002.

Hebdidge, Dick. *Subculture: The Meaning of Style*. London: Methuen, 1979.

Herrnstein Smith, Barbara. *Contingencies of Value*. Cambridge, MA: Harvard University Press, 1988.

Hoy, Suellen. *Chasing Dirt*. Oxford: Oxford University Press, 1995.

Hunter, Ian. "Subjectivity and Government." *Economy and Society* 22, no. 1 (1993): 128.

Jameson, Fredric. *The Seeds of Time*. New York: Columbia University Press, 1994.

Kopytoff, Igor. "The Cultural Biography of Things: Commoditization as Process." In *The Social Life of Things*, edited by Arjun Appadurai. New York: Cambridge University Press, 1986.

Kristeva, Julia. *Powers of Horror.* New York: Columbia University Press, 1982.

Laporte, Dominique. *History of Shit.* Translated by Nadia Benabid and Rodolphe El-Khoury. Cambridge, MA: MIT Press, 2000.

Latour, Bruno. *We Have Never Been Modern.* Cambridge, MA: Harvard University Press, 1993.

Law, John. "Economics as Interference." In du Gay and Pryke, *Cultural Economy.*

Linke, Michael. " Sydney's Sustainable House." *ReNew,* July–September 1997, 14–17.

Lucas, Gavin. "Disposability and Dispossession in the Twentieth Century." *Journal of Material Culture* 7, no. 1 (2002).

Luke, Timothy. "Green Consumerism: Ecology and the Ruse of Recycling." In *In the Nature of Things,* edited by Jane Bennett and William Chaloupka. Minneapolis: University of Minnesota Press, 1993.

Lupton, Ellen, and J. Abbott Miller. *The Bathroom, the Kitchen and the Aesthetics of Waste.* Cambridge, MA: MIT Visual Arts Center, 1992.

Magee, Paul. *From Here to Tierra Del Fuego.* Urbana, University of Illinois Press, 2000.

Marks, Laura. *The Skin of the Film.* Durham, NC: Duke, 2000.

Marx, Karl. *Capital.* Vol. 1. Moscow: Progress, 1971.

Massumi, Brian. *Parables for the Virtual.* Durham, NC: Duke, 2002.

———. "Too Blue: Colour Patch for an Expanded Empiricism." *Cultural Studies* 14, no. 2 (2000): 177–226.

Melosi, Martin. *Garbage in Cities: Refuse, Reform and the Environment, 1880–1980.* Texas: A & M University Press, 1981.

Meuke, Stephen. "A Landscape of Variability." In *Uncertain Ground: Essays between Art and Nature,* edited by Nicholas Thomas. Sydney: Art Gallery of New South Wales, 1999.

Mills, Catherine. "Biopower, Liberal Eugenics and Nihilism." Unpublished paper presented at BIOS—A Politics and Technology Research Workshop, University of New South Wales, August 6, 2004.

North Shore Times. Letters to the editor section, October 16, 1998.

Osborne, Peter. "Small-scale Victories, Large-scale Defeats." In *Destruction and Experience*, edited by Andrew Benjamin and Peter Osborne. Manchester: Clinamen, 2000.

Osborne, Thomas. "Security and Vitality: Drains, Liberalism and Power in the Nineteenth Century." In *Foucault and Political Reason*, edited by Andrew Barry, Thomas Osborne, and Nikolas Rose. Chicago: University of Chicago Press, 1996.

Packard, Vance. *The Waste Makers*. Middlesex, England: Penguin, 1963.

Patton, Paul. *Deleuze and the Political*. London: Routledge, 2000.

Phillips, Adam. *Darwin's Worms*. London: Faber and Faber, 1999.

Poovey, Mary. *Making a Social Body*. Chicago: University of Chicago Press, 1995.

Probyn, Elspeth. *Carnal Appetites*. London: Routledge, 2000.

Rabinow, Paul, ed. *Michel Foucault: Ethics, Subjectivity and Truth*. London: Allen Lane / Penguin, 1997.

Rathje, William, and Cullen Murphy. *Rubbish! The Archaeology of Garbage*. New York: Harper Collins, 2001.

Ross, Andrew. "The Lonely Hour of Scarcity." In *Real Love: In Pursuit of Cultural Justice*. London: Routledge, 1998.

Rutherford, Anne. "The Poetics of a Potato." *Metro Magazine* 137 (2003): 126–31.

Sebald, W.G. *Austerlitz*. London: Penguin, 2001.

Sedgwick, Eve. *Touching Feeling*. Vol. 28. Durham, NC: Duke, 2003.

Serres, Michel. *The Natural Contract*. Ann Arbor: University of Michigan Press, 1995.

Shuttlesworth, Dorothy. *Litter—The Ugly Enemy*. New York: Doubleday, 1973.

Simmel, Georg. *The Philosophy of Money*. London: Routledge, 1978.

Stern, Lesley. "Paths That Wind through the Thicket of Things." *Critical Inquiry* 28 (Autumn 2001).

Strasser, Susan. *Waste and Want: A Social History of Trash*. New York: Metropolitan Books, 1999.

Thompson, Michael. *Rubbish Theory: The Creation and Destruction of Value*. Oxford: Oxford University Press, 1979.

Tierney, John. "Recycling Is Garbage." *New York Times Magazine*, June 30, 1996.

Tierney, Thomas. *The Value of Convenience.* New York: State University of New York Press, 1993.

Warner, Michael. *Publics and Counterpublics.* New York: Zone Books, 2002.

Waste Paper in Australia. Sydney: Ausnewz Pulp and Paper, 1998.

Wood, James. "Black Noise." *New Republic* 217, no. 19 (1997).

About the Author

Gay Hawkins is an associate professor in cultural theory in the School of Media, Film and Theatre at the University of New South Wales, Sydney, Australia. Her most recent book is a coedited collection with Stephen Muecke, *Culture and Waste: The Creation and Destruction of Value* (2002).